The New York Times
Cooking

The New Essentials of French Cooking

MELISSA CLARK

PHOTOGRAPHS BY FRANCESCO TONELLI

CONTENTS

Omelet
8

Quiche
24

Sole Meunière
42

Ratatouille
64

Coq au Vin
69

Steak

84

Tagine

98

Pommes Anna

112

Cassoulet

129

Soufflé

145

A depiction of a Paris provision shop in 1871, from The Illustrated London News.

INTRODUCTION

In the pages that follow, you will find 10 French dishes
for the modern cook to master — the new essentials.

IT'S EASY TO FORGET HOW COMPELLING traditional French cooking can be. Maybe it seems stuffy and old-fashioned, a vestige of an era of tuxedoed waiters and starchy tablecloths.

Yet French food remains the most vibrant and delectable cuisines in the world. It is elegant and rustic, full of regional variety and foundational techniques. And it is influential: The development and codification of a national cuisine in France forever changed the way people around the world think about food.

Choosing the recipes was one of the most difficult parts of the process. I looked for dishes that are not only classic and inherently delicious, but that also help tell the rich story of the depth and breadth of French cooking — for instance, how a simple pan of fried, beaten eggs was gradually refined into the glorious omelet. I also included a tagine, a more contemporary addition to the French kitchen and one that reflects the North African contribution to France's national cuisine. I hope these dishes capture a slice of a culture obsessed with all things culinary.

The recipes themselves are based on classics, but I've incorporated simpler, more intuitive methods. The resulting dishes feel both contemporary and traditional, and are presented here with history and context, information on ingredients, cooking advice and lessons in technique. If you want to try to make a cassoulet, the most ambitious project in these pages, I'll walk you through the entire recipe so that you end up with a stunning meal — and a nuanced understanding of what makes it so wonderfully French.

Omelet

—

om·lit | óm-lit

A dish of beaten eggs cooked in a skillet
with butter and then folded.

Why Master It?

The omelet is the egg taken to its highest form. With nothing more added than salt and the tiniest amount of butter, the omelet celebrates the richness of eggs without distracting from their delicacy.

THE FRENCH HAVE A GENIUS FOR COOKING WITH EGGS. They poach them, they use them in sauces, they whip them into soufflés, they bake them into quiches. And they fold them into omelets, an excellent introduction to that great tradition.

Like much of French cuisine, the omelet represents the perfect intersection of a precise technique and a pristine ingredient. The more skilled the cook and the better the eggs, the more ethereal the result, so practice often.

The omelet is such an icon that it is often held up as the test of a chef's abilities. But it is also one of the fundamentals, among the first dishes Julia Child made on Boston public television for French cooking neophytes as she publicized "Mastering the Art of French Cooking." It is undeniably speedy. As Child once said, "How about dinner in half a minute?"

So what makes an omelet uniquely French? It is the exacting technique of folding the eggs to yield tender, loose curds in the center and a delicate but firm exterior. That juxtaposition sets the omelet apart from Italian frittatas, Spanish tortillas and Persian kukus, which are cooked into flat, sliceable cakes. We give a classic omelet recipe here, and another for an omelet mousseline, a fluffy variation in which the whites are whipped and then added to the yolks.

An omelet can be savory or sweet; though sweet omelets are rare these days, it might be time to resurrect them. After all, eggs can be seasoned with sugar and fruit or a syrupy jam as easily as with salt, onions and cheese: Think of clafoutis, tarts and soufflés. Once you have mastered the basic technique, the variations are practically limitless.

OMELET **11**

Illustration from the French weekly magazine La Cuisine des Familles, 1905.

A Brief History

THE OMELET IS ANCIENT. Doubtlessly humans have eaten fried, beaten eggs since hens and other fowl were domesticated in the sixth century B.C. Romans had ovemele, eggs cooked with honey and pepper; Persians ate kuku, eggs fried with copious amounts of herbs. There were tortillas in early Spain, and frittatas in what would become Italy.

All were fried cakes loaded with fillings—vegetables, meat, potatoes, spices and herbs—cooked on both sides until set, and then sliced so they could be eaten out of hand.

But the fluffy French omelet we know is different. With its barely set eggs, it requires a spoon or fork to be eaten. The word omelet and variations of it date to the mid-16th century—around the same time Catherine de Medici of Italy, who was married to King Henry II of France, is said to have introduced the fork to the French. Historians have speculated that the emergence of the fork and the evolution of the omelet may be intertwined.

By the 17th century, the omelet entered the canon, appearing in La Varenne's "Le Pâtissier François" (1653) as an aumelette. The arrival of better stoves with enclosed fires, in the 18th century, made it easier for cooks to prepare omelets because they could more easily regulate the heat. The omelet's popularity has only grown and endured, making it a staple today around the world in restaurants and home kitchens alike.

Omelet

YIELD 1 SERVING | **TIME** 5 MINUTES

This is a basic French omelet with three eggs: enough for a hearty breakfast or brunch, or a light supper for one. The key is to control the heat so the eggs do not brown, and to whisk the eggs in the skillet so the exterior sets but they remain fluffy inside.

3 large eggs

Large pinch fine sea salt, to taste

Freshly ground black pepper, to taste

1 to 2 teaspoons minced fresh herbs, such as parsley, tarragon, chives or a combination (optional)

1 tablespoon unsalted butter

STEP 1 | Crack eggs into a medium bowl. Add 1 tablespoon water, and salt and pepper. Whisk with a fork until egg whites are incorporated into yolks. Mix in herbs, if using.

STEP 2 | Place an 8- to 9-inch skillet (preferably nonstick or seasoned carbon steel) over high heat. Melt butter until bubbling subsides.

STEP 3 | Pour in egg mixture and reduce heat to medium. With the back of a fork or a heatproof rubber spatula, whisk eggs around the skillet until the bottom begins to set. This takes only a few seconds. Add any fillings, if using.

STEP 4 | Tilt the skillet and either bang or flip egg over itself. Use a fork or spatula if necessary to complete folding in half or thirds. Angle the skillet and a serving plate together, and flip omelet onto plate.

Equipment You'll Need

Any pan with a flat bottom can produce an omelet, but the right tools make a better one. Here are our favorites.

OMELET PAN If you don't own a nonstick pan or a seasoned, carbon-steel omelet pan, now is the time to invest in a good one. It's difficult to master an omelet in a stainless-steel pan or cast-iron skillet; those heavier pans are too hard to maneuver. Buy something easy to handle that adjusts to heat changes quickly.

SPATULA A heat-resistant rubber spatula is an excellent all-purpose kitchen tool. Here, you'll use it for stirring and folding the eggs.

Techniques and Tips

The omelet is extraordinarily simple, so it pays to choose your ingredients smartly and practice the cooking techniques at the stove.

CHOOSING INGREDIENTS

• European-style butter is best for an omelet because the fat content is slightly higher than that of most American-style butters. Always use unsalted butter, then add salt to the eggs, so you have greater control over the seasoning.

• Use good eggs, preferably local. Eggs are the main component of this dish; the more flavorful they are, the better your omelet will be. They should be at room temperature, to allow your omelet to cook quickly and evenly. Leave them on the counter for an hour before cooking, or let them sit covered in warm water for 20 minutes.

NOTES

- Don't overbeat your eggs. Beat them lightly, just until the white and yolks are well mixed and uniform in color, but not airy or bubbly. If you introduce too much air into the eggs by whipping them, you'll end up with something closer to an omelet mousseline (see the next recipe) rather than the classic dish.

- For fluffier eggs, add up to a tablespoon of diced cold butter to the beaten eggs before cooking.

- Use an absolutely clean frying pan. Don't cook the eggs in bacon fat, or any singed leftovers that will alter the look and taste of your omelet.

- Be judicious with the butter in the pan. You just need enough to coat the pan lightly but thoroughly—about 1 tablespoon. Do not use too much, or the eggs will be heavy and greasy rather than light.

- For extra flavor, brown the butter in the pan before adding the eggs.

- For richer eggs, after folding the omelet, smear the top with softened butter or crème fraîche before serving. This is also a good way to get garnishes to stick to the top, caviar and herbs in particular.

COOKING AND FOLDING THE OMELET

You've got three main technique options for cooking an omelet. While all will get you to the same end result of ethereal scrambled eggs encased in a gossamer shell, cooks generally prefer one method over the others. Try them,

NOTES

and see which one works best for you. Note that all are doing the same thing: introducing air into the eggs by beating them until they are fluffy, then letting the bottom set so it holds all those light, eggy curds.

As with any new technique, practice makes all the difference here. So after choosing the method you like best, practice it until you get it just right for your taste. You can fold your omelet either in half or thirds as desired.

1. THE FORK METHOD Pour the eggs into the hot pan, and immediately start beating them with a fork until fluffy. Once curds begin to form, stop beating and let the bottom of the eggs set for a few seconds before tossing the pan or using a fork to fold the eggs over themselves, either in half or thirds.

NOTES

2. THE SWIRL METHOD Pour the eggs into the hot pan, then vigorously swirl the pan, shaking it back and forth to agitate the eggs until the center is fluffy and filled with large curds of eggs, and the bottom sets. Shake some more until the eggs start to flip over themselves, then slide the omelet onto a plate in half, or use a fork or spatula to fold into thirds.

3. THE LIFT METHOD Pour the eggs into the hot pan and let them set for a few seconds. Lift the set edges with a spatula or fork to let uncooked egg run underneath, pushing the cooked part of the eggs into the center of the pan to form large, fluffy curds. Repeat this until the eggs are set on the bottom and just cooked in the center. Then use the spatula or fork to fold the eggs, either in half or in thirds.

Variation: Omelet Mousseline

YIELD 1 SERVING | **TIME** 5 MINUTES

This omelet is fluffier and lighter than the classic version. It uses Auguste Escoffier's technique: Whip the egg whites and fold in the yolks. A small amount of heavy cream enriches the omelet, making it a good candidate for a jam filling or a sprinkle of powdered sugar.

3 large eggs, whites and yolks separated

1 tablespoon heavy cream

Large pinch fine sea salt, to taste

Freshly ground black pepper, to taste

1 tablespoon unsalted butter

STEP 1 | Using an electric mixer, beat egg whites until stiff peaks form. Meanwhile, in a large bowl, beat yolks with heavy cream, salt and pepper. Fold ¼ of stiff egg whites into yolks. Gently fold in remaining whites in two increments.

STEP 2 | Place an 8- to 9-inch skillet over high heat. Melt butter until bubbling subsides.

STEP 3 | Pour in egg mixture; reduce heat to medium. Using a spatula, spread egg mixture to cover the entire skillet and cook until set on the bottom. This takes only a few seconds. Use a spatula to fold egg over itself in half or thirds. Tilt skillet and a serving plate together, and flip omelet onto the plate.

OMELET

Variations: Omelet Fillings

In France, omelets are often served plain, or with a sprinkle of minced herbs. When they are filled, it is with discretion, just enough to complement the flavor of the eggs without overwhelming them. Use ¼ cup to ⅓ cup filling for a three-egg omelet, or less with highly flavorful ingredients like herbs and strong cheeses.

HERBS AND VEGETABLES According to the French chef Jacques Pépin, the classic herbs for omelets are chives, chervil, tarragon and parsley. Add the minced herbs to the bowl along with the eggs and beat everything together. Vegetables of all kinds make great additions to omelets. They all need to be cooked first, in any way you like. Feel free to use leftovers if you have sautéed or roasted vegetables from last night's dinner. Try spinach, kale, mushrooms, onion, shredded zucchini, shredded turnip, broccoli, corn, eggplant, diced cooked potatoes or roasted peppers. Cubed ripe tomato can be added raw, though it is a good idea to seed it first.

MEATS AND SEAFOOD Meat can give an omelet savory heft. Use diced ham or salami; cooked, crumbled sausages; cooked chicken or turkey; browned pancetta or bacon; or diced leftover roasted meats (roast beef or pork or lamb) or leftover stew meats. Even that little bit of leftover beef Bourguignon can find new purpose in life folded into an omelet.

Cooked flaked fish, either left over or freshly prepared, works beautifully in an omelet. Any kind of fish will work, from the lightest, flakiest sole to more robust salmon or sardines. Chopped cooked shrimp and scallops are lovely. You could also use canned fish such as tuna or salmon; flake the fish first and blot away any excess oil with paper towels.

Diced smoked salmon is a more deluxe omelet filling, as is caviar—either pricey sturgeon roe, or more affordable salmon or trout roe. Add caviar to the omelet after cooking, when it is already on the plate, and do so just before serving. It is more of a garnish than a filling. A dollop of crème fraîche or sour cream works particularly well alongside.

CHEESE You can add any kind of cheese to an omelet, both shredded or grated cheeses such as Cheddar, Gruyère, Parmesan or mozzarella, and diced soft cheese, including soft goat cheese or cream cheese, or ripe Brie or Camembert (remove the rind or not, as you please). Crumbled blue cheese or feta also work well.

JAM Jam is nice with either a regular omelet or a mousseline omelet, but skip the black pepper. Use 2 to 3 tablespoons of any flavor jam or fruit compote, then sift powdered sugar over the top of the omelet when done.

Quiche

---

quiche | kēsh
A savory tart of rich egg custard
baked in a pastry shell.

Why Master It?

French pastries are as much a savory tradition as they
are a sweet one, enmeshed in the rhythms of daily life.
That is particularly true of the country's many
onion tarts, of which quiche is the most celebrated.

OF ALL THE SAVORY PASTRIES IN THE FRENCH CANON, from flaky croissants to cheese-laden gougères, tarts are the ones that are made at home just as frequently as they are ordered in restaurants and picked up at takeout shops. You'll find tarts served as a starter for dinner, as the focal point of a light lunch or as a main course at weekend brunch. They come in many styles, with much regional variation. Of all the classics, the elegant quiche is the best known.

The quiche has been a punch line in the past ("real men don't eat quiche"), but that hasn't stopped it from becoming a staple of weekend brunch for a group. And because it can be served warm or at room temperature, you can cook and still enjoy the company.

In its most traditional form, a quiche is composed of a buttery short-crust pastry shell holding a silky egg custard and a savory filling. And although the quiche has gone international, charming its way into North American and British culture, particularly as a brunch staple, the French are the ones who innovated and then perfected the recipe, especially the rich, buttery dough called pâte brisée.

Once you master this dough, you will find that quiche becomes dead simple to make. And you can do so with ingredients you may already have: eggs and cream.

The French treat tarts and quiches as an economical way to use meat or vegetables that are lying around, combining odds and ends into a harmonious result. You will find countless variations in fillings—salmon quiches, eggplant tarts and the like.

Quiches can be the star of a meal, served with a side salad, or can be a wonderful side dish. Cheese, herbs, meats, fish or vegetables make the quiche a chameleon of dishes, as simple or complicated as you want to make it.

But it is the modest onion that often stars in a French tart. Onions are mainstays in French cuisine, flavoring meats and sauces, and soups and stews. But they fare just as well, if not better, on their own, as the main attraction.

Cooked slowly in butter until satiny and soft, onions add flavor and texture to the custard of a classic quiche. Sweet caramelized onions are mixed with anchovies to top the Provençal tart called pissaladière. And minced onions are combined with bacon and fromage blanc (a soft, yogurtlike cheese), then baked pizza-style at high heat, to make a tangy, crunchy tarte flambée, popular in Alsace and the surrounding area. Each tart highlights onions in a different way, and they're all worth taking the time to get to know.

"Still Life With a Pie" by Clara Peeters, c. 1611.

A Brief History

SAVORY OPEN-FACED TARTS ARE DERIVED FROM PIES, which were known to have been baked in ancient Egypt and Rome, though the tradition most likely goes back much further.

That crust was merely a vessel for containing the fillings while they baked. The whole pie wasn't meant to be eaten — just its contents, which could be as simple as ground meat and potatoes, or as elaborate as scores of roasted quail or pheasants, even whole, stuffed lambs.

Since the pastry was not meant to be consumed, it tended to be coarse and unappetizing, though when it was soaked in meat juices after baking, it became palatable enough for the servants. There was even a trade in selling leftover pastry to the poor, who gathered outside castles and estates to wait for crusts to gnaw on.

Open-faced tarts were a medieval innovation, dating roughly to the 14th century. These tarts could be made savory or sweet (or sometimes both, in the best medieval tradition), and were baked with a more delicate pastry meant to be delicious. In France, tarts made with the dough known as pâte brisée were cataloged in La Varenne's "Le Patissier François" (1653).

The egg and bacon tart we know today as quiche Lorraine originated in the area of the same name, in northeast France, where culture and cuisine were highly influenced by neighboring Germany. (Quiche itself was most likely derived from German kuchen; that may also be the source of its name.) It dates to the early 19th century, though its variations, including quiche aux oignons, did not become popular around France until the early 20th century.

Then there is tarte flambée (also known as flammekueche), the yeasted tart made with onion, bacon and fromage blanc, from neighboring Alsace. And the south of France is home to pissaladière, a thin, square, pizzalike dish topped with onions, anchovies, olives and herbs. Its name comes from pissala, an anchovy and sardine purée made from locally caught and salted fish — a briny regional flavor that shines alongside the sweetness of the onions.

Onion Quiche

YIELD 8 SERVINGS | **TIME** 2½ HOURS

Sweet bits of onion suffuse this tart, which gets its brawny, salty tang from browned chunks of cured pork (lardons, pancetta or bacon). Both delicate and rich, it makes a lovely lunch or brunch dish, one best served warm or at room temperature on the day you baked it.

FOR THE CRUST

2 cups/250 grams all-purpose flour, more as needed

1 teaspoon kosher salt

¼ teaspoon sugar

1 cup/225 grams unsalted butter (2 sticks), cold, cut in ½-inch cubes

Scant ½ cup ice water, or as needed

FOR THE FILLING

4 tablespoons/56 grams unsalted butter

1 tablespoon extra-virgin olive oil

2½ pounds/1.1 kilograms onions (about 6 to 8 large), finely chopped

1½ tablespoons all-purpose flour

(continued on page 32)

STEP 1 | Make the tart dough: In a food processor, pulse flour, salt and sugar to combine. Add butter, then pulse until lima-bean-size pieces form. Gradually drizzle water into mixture and pulse just to combine, adding more water by the tablespoon if dough doesn't come together. Transfer dough to a lightly floured surface. Press it together into a ball, flatten into a disk and wrap in plastic. Refrigerate for at least 1 hour and up to 3 days. (If you don't have a food processor, see Tip on page 34.)

STEP 2 | While dough chills, cook the onions for the filling: In a 12-inch skillet over medium heat, melt 3 tablespoons of the butter and the oil. Add onions and cook, stirring occasionally, until pale golden and liquid has been cooked off, about 1 hour. (If the onions start to get too dark, reduce the heat to low.) Stir in flour and cook for an additional 5 minutes. Remove from heat.

STEP 3 | Butter a 9-inch tart pan. Take chilled dough out of plastic wrap and place on a floured surface. Roll dough into an 11-inch circle, drape it over tart pan and press into bottom edges and down sides. Use a knife or rolling pin to cut off excess dough, then use your fingers to push dough ¼-inch up past the edge of pan. Use a fork to poke evenly

QUICHE **31**

Onion Quiche | CONTINUED

2 ounces/57 grams lardons, diced pancetta or bacon (about ½ cup)

2 large eggs

⅔ cup/158 milliliters heavy cream

1 teaspoon kosher salt

¼ teaspoon freshly ground black pepper

¼ teaspoon freshly grated nutmeg

2 ounces Gruyère, shredded (about ½ cup)

spaced holes in the bottom and sides of the dough and chill for 30 minutes.

STEP 4 | Heat oven to 400 degrees. Place chilled tart on a baking sheet. Line with foil, fill with pie weights and bake for 15 minutes. Remove tart from oven and carefully remove foil and pie weights. Return tart to oven to continue baking, uncovered, until dough is just baked through and barely turning golden on the edges, about 5 minutes. Remove from oven and let cool to room temperature. Reduce oven temperature to 375 degrees.

STEP 5 | Prepare lardons: Heat a medium, dry skillet over medium heat, then add lardons and cook until they start to brown, about 8 minutes. Use a slotted spoon to transfer to a plate lined with a paper towel.

STEP 6 | In a large bowl, whisk to combine eggs, cream, salt, pepper and nutmeg. Fold in onions, then half the Gruyère. Cube remaining 1 tablespoon butter into pea-size pieces.

STEP 7 | Scatter cooked lardons over parbaked tart shell. Scrape egg and onion mixture into shell, smoothing top, and then scatter remaining Gruyère on top. Dot with butter pieces, then bake in a 375-degree oven until puffed and browned, 25 to 30 minutes. Let cool slightly, then remove tart ring from pan and slide quiche onto a wire rack. Serve warm or at room temperature.

Equipment You'll Need

Since quiche is really just a pie, you can use mostly the same equipment. But you definitely want a tart pan with a removable ring.

QUICHE OR TART PAN It's best to use a 9-inch metal pan with a removable bottom. While you can use a glass or ceramic quiche pan, you won't be able to remove the quiche from the pan before serving. It's also smart to place the pan on a baking sheet before it goes into the oven. This helps distribute the heat, which cooks the quiche evenly, and it eliminates the chance the pan will leak in your oven.

FOOD PROCESSOR Dough comes together quickly in a food processor, but take care not to overprocess it. A pastry cutter is inexpensive and works well, too; some people prefer it because using one makes it much harder to overwork the dough. If you don't have either, use your fingers to work the butter into the dough.

ROLLING PIN French rolling pins tend to be made of one solid, smooth piece of wood, and often have tapered ends. But you can use any kind of rolling pin you've got—or even a wine bottle in a pinch.

PIE WEIGHTS Empty tart crusts are often prebaked (a process known as blind baking) before they are filled and returned to the oven to finish. This gives you a browned crust that won't get soggy. Weights keep the dough from shrinking as it bakes. If you don't have them, use rice, dried beans or pennies (rinse in soapy water and dry them first).

Techniques and Tips

The secrets to a successful onion quiche: a flaky butter crust and pale, tender onions in the custard filling.

MAKING THE DOUGH

- High-fat European-style butter produces the flakiest crust. Many specialty food stores carry it. If you can find it, it's worth the extra cost.

- Always make sure that the butter is cold when you start, and that the dough stays cold as you work with it. If it starts to soften at any time, put it back in the refrigerator to firm up.

- To prepare the dough without a food processor, use a pastry cutter or a knife and fork to cut butter into flour mixture. Stir in water until dough just comes together into a ball. Cut dough into 4 pieces, and use the heel of your hand to smear one piece away from you on the work surface so it spreads about 6 inches. Gather that piece, place it to the side and repeat with remaining pieces of dough. Press to combine all the smeared pieces into a flat disk, wrap in plastic and chill.

- When you cut the butter into the flour, either by hand or by using the food processor, you want lima-bean-size pieces of butter. These big pieces of butter will make the dough flaky; as they melt in the oven, they release steam, which creates air pockets. These air pockets are the flakes that make a light and crisp crust. (This is also why you want to keep the butter cold as you work with the dough. It ensures that the butter won't melt into the flour as you blend it, but will stay in distinct pieces.)

- As you roll the dough, keep it moving around on your countertop, flipping it over and adding more flour if it starts to stick. By flipping and moving it around as you roll, you avoid rolling it into your countertop and having to add too much flour. (Too much flour can make the dough dry and tough.)

- Use a sharp knife to trim the excess dough from the ring. It can also press the dough into the fluted pan.

- Chill the dough after you roll it out and fit it into the pan. This firms it up before baking, which keeps the dough from shrinking too much in the oven's heat.

PREPARING THE ONIONS
- Choose large white or Spanish onions with high water content and some bite. Avoid sweet onions such as Vidalias, which could make the tart cloying.

- The onions are cooked slowly and gently, so they don't take on too much color. Make sure to use enough butter and oil to cover the bottom of the pan before you add the onions. You need to smother your onions in the fat so they remain pale and turn very soft. An hour may sound like a long time, but low and slow is the best way to go here.

NOTES

QUICHE 35

NOTES

- If the onions start to brown, turn down the heat a little, from medium to medium-low. Stir them around often, and scrape up any lightly browned bits on the bottom or sides of the pan so the browning doesn't spread.

- Adding a tablespoon or two of flour to the onions helps thicken the quiche filling, and it also reduces sogginess after baking. Sprinkle flour over the onions at least 5 minutes before they are done cooking, so the raw flavor in the flour will be cooked out.

BAKING AND SERVING

- In an ideal world, serve your quiche within an hour of baking, while it's still. But you can assemble and bake within six hours of serving.

- Always let the quiche cool for at least 20 minutes on a wire rack (which lets air circulate around the pan) before trying to remove from the pan. This is both to avoid burning yourself, and to allow the pastry to set.

- The dough and onions can be made up to 3 days ahead and chilled. You can even prebake the crust the day before; keep it at room temperature, covered.

- Don't refrigerate your quiche if you can avoid it. It leads to soggy pastry.

- To reheat a room-temperature quiche before serving, let it warm, uncovered, in a 300-degree oven for 10 to 20 minutes. (If it has been in the refrigerator, add another 10 minutes or so.)

Variations: Quiche Fillings

Feel free to play with fillings and flavors, swapping in ingredients as you like to make a quiche more (or less) robust. Just be sure to keep the custard ratios the same: 1 egg to ⅓ cup heavy cream.

HERBS AND OLIVES Add 1 to 2 tablespoons chopped fresh herbs to the onion quiche recipe above to give it freshness and verve. Basil, thyme, cilantro, chervil or chives work nicely. You could also add ¼ cup chopped pitted black or green olives, in place of the herbs or in addition to them.

CHEESE Substitute other cheese for the Gruyère, including Cheddar, blue cheese, feta, manchego, Gouda or firm goat cheese. Or you could eliminate the cheese entirely if you prefer.

SMOKED FISH Skip the bacon or pancetta and add 1 to 2 ounces smoked fish to the quiche instead. You don't need to brown the fish first; just dice it and scatter over the pre-baked crust in place of the lardons. Smoked salmon, white fish and trout are all great options.

VEGETABLES Substitute 1½ to 2 cups of other cooked vegetables for the onions. Good candidates include sautéed spinach or chard; roasted or sautéed mushrooms, eggplant or zucchini; or roasted tomatoes or butternut squash.

Variation: Tarte Flambée

YIELD 8 SERVINGS | **TIME** 40 MINUTES

Here is another onion tart from the French tradition, a baker's treat that used the yeasted dough left over from making bread. It was topped with onions, bacon and fromage blanc, and baked until the dough puffed and the onions singed at the edges. This version uses a biscuitlike crust instead, adapted from the chef Gabriel Kreuther. Serve this as an appetizer or a light main course, or for brunch.

¼ cup crème fraîche

⅓ cup fromage blanc

⅛ teaspoon freshly grated nutmeg

1 teaspoon kosher salt, more to taste

Freshly ground black pepper, to taste

⅞ cup/110 grams all-purpose flour, plus more for dusting

1½ teaspoons baking powder

1½ teaspoons olive oil

1 large egg yolk

2 strips/100 grams thick-cut smoked bacon, finely diced (about ⅔ cup)

⅓ cup finely chopped white onion

STEP 1 | If you have a pizza stone, place it on the middle rack of your oven, top with a baking sheet, and heat the oven to 425 degrees. (If you don't have a stone, just place the baking sheet on the oven rack).

STEP 2 | In a medium bowl, combine crème fraîche, fromage blanc, nutmeg, ½ teaspoon salt and the pepper. Set aside while you make the dough.

STEP 3 | In a separate medium bowl, whisk to combine flour, baking powder and remaining ½ teaspoon salt. In a small bowl, whisk to combine olive oil, egg yolk and ¼ cup water. Add to dry ingredients and use a fork to combine until it creates a shaggy dough.

STEP 4 | Turn the dough out onto a floured surface and knead for 1 minute, until the dough is uniform and elastic. (Flour your hands as necessary to keep the dough from sticking.) Roll out to a 12-inch round, then transfer to a parchment-lined baking sheet without a rim (or use an overturned rimmed baking pan).

STEP 5 | Spread fromage blanc mixture evenly over the dough, leaving a ½-inch border along the edges. Sprinkle bacon

and onions over fromage blanc. Slide tart, still on parchment paper, off baking sheet and directly onto baking sheet in oven.

STEP 6 | Bake until top is beginning to brownand sides are golden and crispy, about 20 minutes. Remove from oven and slide off parchment paper to serving platter. Serve warm.

Adapted From Gabriel Kreuther

Variation: Pissaladière

YIELD 8 SERVINGS | **TIME** 2½ HOURS

Caramelized onions, briny anchovies and olives make up the topping for this Provençal tart. Our version calls for a yeasted dough, making it somewhat like a pizza. Pissaladière makes great picnic fare, in addition to being a terrific appetizer or lunch dish.

FOR THE FILLING

18 anchovy fillets, or to taste

¼ cup olive oil

3 pounds/about 1.4 kilograms onions, thinly sliced

1 clove garlic, grated on a Microplane or minced

1 teaspoon thyme leaves, chopped

½ teaspoon fine sea salt

¼ cup Niçoise olives, pitted, or to taste

FOR THE DOUGH

1½ teaspoons active dry yeast

⅔ cup warm water

3 tablespoons olive oil

2 cups/250 grams all-purpose flour

1½ teaspoons fine sea salt

STEP 1 | Make the filling: Finely chop 2 of the anchovy fillets. Heat oil in a large skillet over medium heat. Add onions, garlic, thyme and chopped anchovy, then cover pan and cook, stirring occasionally, for 20 minutes. Reduce heat to medium-low, stir in salt, and continue cooking for 25 minutes, stirring occasionally. The onions should be pale golden and very soft; lower the heat if they start to turn dark brown at the edges or stick to the skillet. Remove from heat and cool completely before using.

STEP 2 | Meanwhile, make the dough: In a medium bowl, sprinkle dry yeast over warm water. Let stand until foamy, about 5 minutes, then add oil. In a large bowl, whisk together flour and salt, then stir in yeast mixture with a wooden spoon until combined. Turn bowl's contents out onto a floured surface and knead until uniform and elastic, 3 to 5 minutes. (Flour your hands if necessary to keep dough from sticking.) Transfer dough to an oiled bowl, flip the dough over, cover bowl with a damp cloth and let rest in a draft-free place for 1 hour.

STEP 3 | Lightly oil an 11 x 17-inch rimmed baking sheet. Working on a floured surface, roll dough into an 11 x 16-inch rectangle, then transfer it to the oiled baking sheet and press the dough to the sides. Cover with a damp cloth and let dough rest for 30 minutes.

STEP 4 | Heat the oven to 400 degrees. Spread cooked onions evenly over dough, and top with remaining anchovies and olives. Bake until edges and underside are golden brown, 20 to 25 minutes. Serve warm or at room temperature.

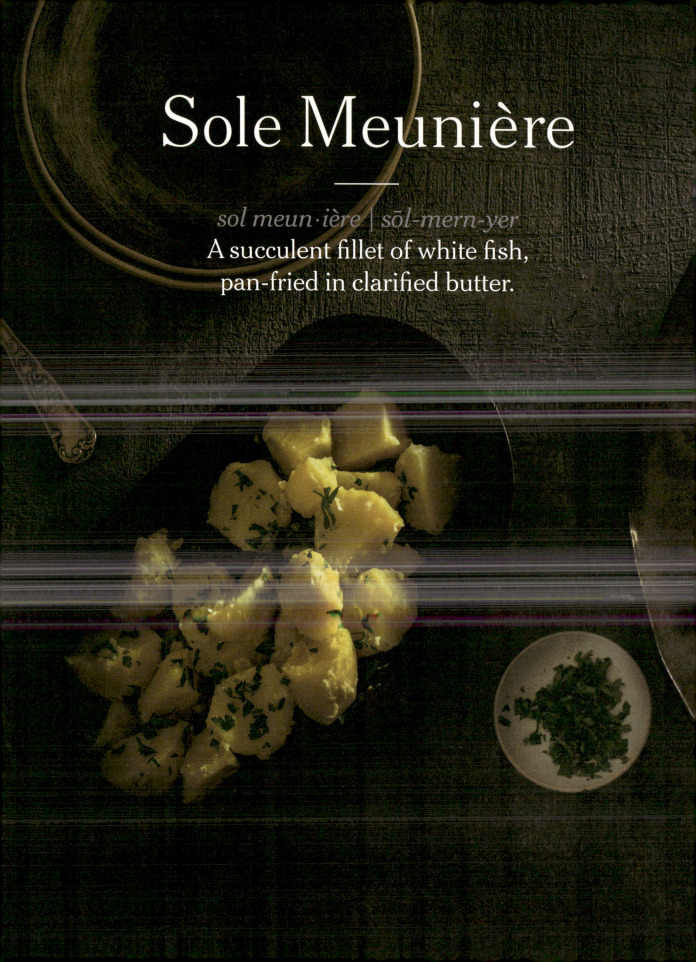

Sole Meunière

sol meun·ière | *sōl-mern-yer*

A succulent fillet of white fish,
pan-fried in clarified butter.

Why Master It?

Here is the dish that made Julia Child fall in love with French cuisine: delicate fish fillets, lightly sautéed and covered with browned butter. She declared her first bite "a morsel of perfection." Once you have had sole meunière, you will see why.

THE FRENCH EXCEL AT EXQUISITELY WROUGHT AND TECHNICALLY CHALLENGING FISH DISHES, like bouillabaisse and lobster Thermidor. However, they are just as enamored of simpler recipes that focus on preserving the pristine beauty of their seafood. Sole meunière is a perfect example.

To prepare it, sole, a succulent, flat white fish, is pan-fried in butter until crisp-edged and tender, then served with brown butter pan sauce, a sprinkling of parsley and a lemon wedge. (The term meunière, "in the style of the miller's wife," refers to the flour the fish is dredged in before frying.) Except for the browning of the butter, the ingredients are in their most elemental form, yet together they create a dish of incomparable harmony and depth.

In its most traditional presentation, sole meunière is made with the whole fish, then filleted tableside. But for the most part, home cooks use sole fillets, which makes the process faster and easier—and only slightly less flavorful and juicy than when the fish is cooked on the bone.

Unlike much classic French cuisine, sole meunière requires almost no advance preparation and very little time at the stove. It is a quick way to get to dinner. You probably have flour, salt, pepper, butter and lemon on hand. All you need is a beautiful piece of fish.

That fish does not have be Dover sole, especially given that in recent years, its sustainability has become an issue (not to mention that it is very expensive). Other flat, white, flaky fish will cook up nearly as well, and will taste delightful when pan-fried and smothered in brown butter. After all, there are very few things that wouldn't.

"Pleuronectes solea, the sole," c. 1785."

A Brief History

WITH OVER 100 CATALOGED PREPARATIONS, sole is one of the most esteemed fish in French cuisine, and sole meunière is the signature dish. It is the plainness of the recipe that makes it seem at once universal and utterly French. Almost all coastal cultures have some version of lightly fried fish, but only in France is it smothered in brown butter.

Little is known about how sole meunière came to be, though we do know that for at least the past century it's been a specialty of Normandy. "Le Guide Culinaire," by Auguste Escoffier, which was first published in 1903, lists several variations of the dish, including sole meunière with eggplant, with grapes, with cucumbers and with various kinds of mushrooms. However, it is likely that the dish is much older, since it is so very basic.

Sole meunière has long been an extravagance, a costly fixture on the menus of many fine French restaurants. That is because it is traditionally made with Dover sole, a flat fish with delicate and buttery white meat, which separates easily from the bones.

It is that combination of simplicity and luxury that makes it compelling. Elaborate adornments are not necessary, as was made clear in an edition of "Larousse Gastronomique" from the early 20th century: "Sometimes the serving of fish cooked à la meunière is decorated with slices, or half-slices, of lemon, rounds of radish, cutout pieces of beetroot and sprigs of parsley. This kind of ornament is quite useless and not at all in keeping with the recipe."

Today, most French cooks would agree that you need nothing more on top of your buttery sole than a lemon wedge and a hint of parsley. That is the easiest lesson you can learn from French cooking: When you have perfect ingredients, less is more.

Sole Meunière

YIELD 6 SERVINGS | **TIME** 20 MINUTES

Sole meunière highlights the simple flavors of fresh fish, butter, lemon and parsley. Fish is the center of the dish, so using a quality fillet is important. The fish is pan-fried in clarified butter, which can take on heat without browning; a recipe follows.

½ cup all-purpose flour

6 4-ounce skinless, boneless sole or other thin fish fillets, patted dry

Kosher salt, to taste

Freshly ground white or black pepper, to taste

4 tablespoons clarified butter

4 tablespoons unsalted butter, diced, at room temperature

3 tablespoons minced parsley

1 lemon, cut into wedges, for serving

STEP 1 | Heat oven to 200 degrees and place a large oven-safe plate or baking sheet inside.

STEP 2 | Place flour on a large, shallow plate. Season both sides of fish fillets with salt and pepper to taste. Dredge fish in flour, shaking off excess.

STEP 3 | In a 12-inch nonstick or enamel-lined skillet over medium-high heat, heat 2 tablespoons clarified butter until bubbling. Place half of the fish fillets in the pan and cook until just done, 2 to 3 minutes per side, then transfer to the plate or baking sheet in the oven to keep warm. Add 2 more tablespoons clarified butter to skillet and heat until bubbling, then cook remaining fillets. Wipe out the skillet.

STEP 4 | Arrange the fish on a warm serving platter. Top with parsley. In reserved skillet, heat 4 tablespoons unsalted butter until bubbling and golden, 1 to 2 minutes, then pour evenly over fillets. Serve immediately, with lemon wedges on the side.

Clarified Butter

YIELD 12 TABLESPOONS, OR ¾ CUP | **TIME** 10 MINUTES

Clear, golden clarified butter can withstand heat without burning for a longer period and at a higher temperature, making it ideal for pan-frying. The process is simple and takes just a few minutes.

1 cup unsalted butter (2 sticks)

STEP 1 | In a small pot, melt butter over low heat until bubbling and foaming subsides. Remove from heat, let cool slightly (don't let butter resolidify), then skim any foam off the top.

STEP 2 | Line a sieve with cheesecloth or a clean dish towel and place over a heat-safe bowl or container. Leaving the white milk solids at the bottom of the pot, carefully pour or spoon yellow butter fat through the sieve and into the container. Let cool completely before refrigerating for up to 1 month.

Equipment You'll Need

The theme of simplicity continues with what you need to make sole meunière: not much.

SKILLET Use a 12-inch skillet, which should be large enough to fit the length of your fish. A heavy-duty nonstick or well-seasoned cast-iron pan will help keep the fillets from sticking, making them easier to flip and keep whole. But a stainless steel pan is fine if you're careful when flipping.

SPATULA A tapered fish spatula makes flipping delicate fillets a bit easier, but any spatula will work.

Techniques and Tips

Sole meunière is the kind of recipe that moves quickly once you start cooking, so it's best to give it your full attention. Have the ingredients ready before you begin.

• Use good butter: European-style butter with a high fat content (at least 82 percent) works best here because it contains less moisture than regular butter.

• If you don't want to clarify your butter, use a combination of oil and regular butter instead. You will end up with a more neutral and less buttery flavor, but the recipe will still work. (If you decide not to clarify, then it is especially important to use that high-fat, European-style butter.) Or you could use ghee, which is basically clarified butter in which the milk solids have been allowed to brown before being removed. It has a lightly caramelized, nutty flavor.

• Patting the fish dry before dredging helps the flour cling evenly to the fillet, rather than clump in the damp spots.

• Season the fish itself rather than seasoning the flour. This gives you more precision and control over the seasoning.

NOTES

NOTES

- In classic sole meunière, white pepper is used partly for aesthetics. If you want to use black pepper, that's fine.

- Keep an eye on the fish: When it has finishing cooking, it should be opaque, tender and not too firm. Plunge your fork into the thickest part of the fillet. There should be no resistance. That's how you will know it's done.

- Set your oven to its lowest temperature, and use it to keep the first round of fish warm. This is an easy way to make sure dinner comes to the table at the right temperature. Placing the just-cooked fish on a warm plate before it goes into the oven helps, too.

Variations

Sole meunière is the most basic of dishes to prepare, which makes it easy to swap the fish or augment the seasonings to suit your taste.

FISH You don't need Dover sole to make this dish delectable. Instead, look for local, sustainable, flaky, mild white-fleshed fillets with a mild flavor. Other varieties of sole (including winter sole and lemon sole), halibut and flounder will work well. Or try scrod, cod, hake, trout, salmon, bass, swordfish, sardines or blackfish.

HERBS & SPICES Add a pinch or two of minced sturdy herbs like rosemary, thyme or savory, or ground spices such as cumin, coriander, paprika or curry powder, to the brown butter as it's simmering. Go easy on the spices to let the dish shine.

VEGETABLES If you want to make the dish more substantial, add cooked vegetables to the pan with the butter. Diced sautéed cucumber, shallot or onion, wilted spinach, grated zucchini, cubed eggplant or mushrooms would all do nicely.

GARNISH For a slightly more elaborate garnish that won't overwhelm the flavors of the dish, substitute other soft, leafy herbs for the parsley. Basil, tarragon, coriander and chives are good candidates. Other citrus, such as Meyer lemon, lime, grapefruit or sour orange wedges, can stand in for the usual lemon.

Ratatouille

rat·at·oui·lle | ra-ta-tōo'-ee
A fragrant stew of eggplant, tomatoes, zucchini, onions and peppers.

Why Master It?

The French have a genius for cooking with vegetables. Even the humblest onion is transformed into something glorious in the hands of a Gallic cook. Ratatouille, one of jewels of Provençal cooking, is a fine example of that tradition.

VEGETABLES ARE THE BEDROCK OF FRENCH CUISINE, the foundation upon which all is built. Although cooking bibles like "The Escoffier Cookbook" and "Larousse Gastronomique" may not have as many recipes centering on artichokes and carrots as they do on chicken or beef, it is only because vegetables suffuse the canon and the kitchen, from the broths and sauces that serve as the base of elaborate dishes, to the garnishes that finish them.

But there are a handful of dishes where vegetables are the stars. Ratatouille is beloved for its silky, olive oil-imbued vegetables, which are saturated with the summery scents of garlic and herbs. By mastering this simple but lengthy recipe, you will gain not only deeper insights into how to cook the vegetables in the recipe, but you will also be able to apply that knowledge to other vegetables, making you a better cook all around.

Unlike much of French cuisine, ratatouille does not have a set recipe or precise technique. There are as many versions as there are cooks, each slightly different in method and ingredients.

The most traditional recipes call for cooking each vegetable separately in a pot on the stove until well browned, layering everything back into the pot with a generous amount of olive oil and some tomatoes, and then letting it all slowly stew. Most cooks agree that this is the best way to ensure that the vegetables are cooked to perfection before all are combined, and the flavors left to meld. Try it to see if you agree.

However, all that standing at the stove stirring vegetables can become tedious. Even "Larousse Gastronomique" discards that method in its official recipe, throwing everything into the same pan in stages without the benefit of that individual browning.

But there is another way around the tedium: Use your oven. This is what many contemporary French cooks do, and it's the method our recipe uses. All the vegetables are bathed in olive oil and roasted separately on baking pans until well browned. Then they're mixed together in one pan, covered with more oil and some tomato, and cooked again until everything condenses in flavor, soaking up the good oil and tomato almost like a confit.

That time spent steeping in good oil makes ratatouille one of the rare vegetable dishes that improves as it sits. It is best made in advance, and you can be flexible with the way you cook it, roasting the vegetables in stages as time allows, then combining them all even days later. It is also wonderfully versatile at the table, making a fine starter, side dish or main course, one that can be eaten warm, at room temperature or cold.

"Still Life With Flowers and Vegetables" attributed to Caravaggio (1571–1610)

A Brief History

A SLOWLY COOKED STEW OF EGGPLANT, onions, peppers, summer squash and tomatoes has been simmering on hearths around the Mediterranean since the 16th century, when tomatoes, peppers and squash from the Americas met the eggplant, onion and olive oil already in residence.

This basic combination of summer vegetables takes different forms throughout the region. In Catalonia, it is simmered until it is almost jamlike and called samfaina. In Turkey, it is known as turlu and may also contain potatoes, okra and green beans. Lebanon, Egypt and Greece all have versions. In Provence, it is scented with herbs and garlic and called ratatouille.

The term, which came into use in the 19th century, is derived from the French verbs ratouiller and tatouiller, both meaning to stir up. And the pleasing, percussive-sounding word captures the essence of this dish: a stirring of several vegetables that have been cooked separately before being combined and cooked again to meld their flavors.

Originally, a ratatouille could be any kind of simple or coarse stew. It could include meat, or it could do without it. Nineteenth-century French military slang referred to the dish as a "rata." The first written mentions of the all-vegetable stew from Nice that we know today, also called sauté à la Niçoise, came in the early 20th century.

But by 1930, ratatouille had become entrenched in the Provençal repertoire and quickly gained popularity. Henri Heyraud, the author of "La Cuisine à Nice," described it as a ragoût of eggplant, zucchini, peppers and tomatoes. The use of the word ragoût here is fitting: It means to revive the taste, which is exactly what ratatouille does, giving cooked vegetables and herbs new verve when they are combined and cooked again.

As Provençal cuisine became fashionable all over France (and to a lesser degree in Britain and the United States) in the latter part of the 20th century, the popularity of ratatouille grew. It has since become a summer staple to serve with simple grilled meats, or as a main course in its own right, with the requisite bottle of rosé.

Ratatouille

YIELD 8 TO 10 SERVINGS | **TIME** 3 HOURS

In our version of this classic Provençal dish, vegetables are covered in olive oil and roasted separately, then together, until they collapse into a soft, herb-scented stew. Ratatouille takes time to prepare and tastes better the next day, so plan ahead. For that reason, it's an ideal make-ahead dish for a gathering.

4 garlic cloves

2 medium white onions

3 medium zucchinis

2 medium eggplants

3 sweet red peppers, such as bell peppers, red cubanelle or any other sweet variety

3 sprigs fresh rosemary

6 sprigs fresh thyme

1 cup olive oil, more as needed

2 large heirloom or beefsteak tomatoes

2 small bay leaves, ripped in half

1½ teaspoons fine sea salt, more as needed

Freshly ground black pepper

STEP 1 | Heat oven to 350 degrees.

STEP 2 | Prepare the vegetables: Smash and peel 3 garlic cloves, reserving the 4th. Halve onions through their roots, and slice halves into ¼-inch-thick pieces. Slice zucchini into ¼-inch-thick rounds. Cut eggplant into 1-inch cubes or spears. Seed peppers, and cut them into ¼-inch-thick strips.

STEP 3 | Spread each vegetable on a separate rimmed baking sheet (use extra sheets as necessary). Add the 3 cloves of smashed garlic to the onion pan. Add 1 sprig rosemary and 2 sprigs thyme to each of the pepper, eggplant and zucchini pans. Sprinkle salt lightly over vegetables. Drizzle 3 tablespoons olive oil on each of the pans.

STEP 4 | Place all the pans in the oven (or work in batches if they don't fit at once). Cook until vegetables are very tender and lightly browned at the edges. This will take about 35 to 40 minutes for the peppers (their skins should shrivel), 40 to 45 minutes for the eggplant and zucchini (the eggplant should crisp slightly and the zucchini should be well cooked, so let them go 3 to 5 minutes longer than you normally might), and 60 to 65 minutes for the onions. Don't worry about the vegetables being pretty; they will meld into the ratatouille.

Ratatouille | CONTINUED

Shake or stir the pans every 15 to 20 minutes or so, especially the onions, to assure they roast evenly.

STEP 5 | In the meantime, prepare the tomatoes: Bring a large pot of water to a boil. Add tomatoes and blanch until the skins split, about 10 seconds. Use a slotted spoon to quickly transfer the tomatoes to a bowl filled with ice water.

STEP 6 | Using a paring knife, peel the cooled tomatoes (the skins should slip right off). Halve tomatoes across their equators. Set a sieve over a bowl. Working over the bowl, use your fingers to seed the tomatoes, letting the seeds catch in the sieve and the juice run into the bowl. Discard seeds but save juices. Dice tomatoes and add to the juices in the bowl.

STEP 7 | Finely grate or mince the remaining garlic clove. Add the garlic to the tomatoes along with bay leaves and a large pinch of salt. Set aside.

STEP 8 | Once vegetables are done cooking, combine them on one baking sheet or a large shallow baking dish and add ingredients from tomato bowl. Toss well. Vegetables will be stacked, and that's O.K. Cover generously with olive oil, using remaining ¼ cup oil or more, and sprinkle with salt. Everything should have a good coat of oil, but should not be drowning in it. Cook at least 1 hour, stirring every 15 to 20 minutes, until vegetables are very tender and imbued with juices and oil. Add salt and pepper to taste, then serve warm, or let cool.

Equipment You'll Need

The key to perfect ratatouille is in the quality of the vegetables. But the right tools make cooking easier.

NOTES

SHARP KNIVES You'll need a chef's knife and paring knife to prepare the vegetables. And a well-sharpened knife will make all that chopping go noticeably faster than a dull knife.

BAKING SHEETS The vegetables in this ratatouille are roasted individually before they are all combined. Ideally, you will have at least four large rimmed metal baking sheets for doing so. You can get away with fewer, but you still need to cook the vegetables in batches.

LARGE BAKING DISH You could heap all of the vegetables onto a baking sheet when it is time to cook them together. But a large, shallow, attractive casserole that can travel straight to the table is an appealing way to serve the dish.

Techniques and Tips

Ratatouille is a freer and easier recipe than much of what you'll find in the canon of French cuisine, requiring you to spend more time choosing the ingredients than actually fiddling with them. That said, some techniques can help you get the most deeply flavored dish.

BLANCHING AND PEELING THE TOMATOES

Blanching tomatoes helps loosen the skin, making them easier to peel without losing any of their precious, sweet juices. The trick is remove them from the boiling water before their flesh is cooked. You want to cook only the skin.

Choose tomatoes that are ripe but still firm; soft tomatoes won't hold up to the blanching and peeling. You can use any variety as long as it is flavorful and sweet. However, using large round tomatoes rather than small plum tomatoes makes the blanching, peeling and seeding go more quickly.

RATATOUILLE **63**

NOTES

To begin, bring a medium pot of water to a boil. One at a time, drop the whole tomatoes into the boiling water. Cover and let boil for 10 seconds. Using a slotted spoon or tongs, immediately remove the tomatoes from the pot and plunge them into a bowl of ice water to stop the cooking. Hold a cooled tomato in your hand and use a small paring knife to cut out the stem. From there, you can start to peel the skin. It should slip right off.

Cut each peeled tomato in half around its equator. Set up a bowl with a mesh sieve sitting on top. Squeeze the tomato halves over the sieve so the seeds are caught in the mesh and the juices pool in the bowl. The seeds should slip out easily, but you can use your fingers to pry any stubborn ones from the tomato flesh. Discard the seeds in the sieve. Dice the tomato pulp and add it to the bowl with their juices.

COOKING AND SERVING

• When you are making ratatouille, the quality of the olive oil is as important as that of the vegetables. Make sure to choose a good extra-virgin oil, preferably from France. You'll be using a lot of it here.

• If you don't have four baking sheets, roast the vegetables on individual sheets in succession. Transfer the cooked vegetables to a bowl as they finish cooking. Likewise, if you can't fit all of the baking sheets into your oven at once, cook them in batches.

NOTES

• If your ratatouille emerges from the oven with a lot of excess liquid in the pan, pour the liquid into a saucepan and reduce it over the stove. Then add it back to the dish once it is reduced, to take advantage of its flavor.

• Try the traditional method: Instead of roasting each vegetable on baking sheets, cook them on the stovetop. Heat your largest skillet on the stove, adding a film of oil, and cook each vegetable separately (and the onions, smashed garlic and herbs together). Cook in batches if necessary, so as not to crowd the pan. (If you crowd the pan, the vegetables will steam rather than brown, and will cook unevenly.) As the vegetables soften and brown, transfer them to a bowl. (You can add all the different cooked vegetables to the same bowl.) Add more oil with each batch of vegetables, and season with salt and pepper as you go. When all of the vegetables are cooked, transfer them back to the skillet, along with the tomatoes, grated garlic and a good dose of olive oil. Simmer, uncovered, until they meld together, about 30 to 45 minutes.

• You can make this dish in stages, if that suits your schedule. Roast the vegetables separately a day or two before combining them, and then refrigerate them. When you are ready to return to them, combine with the tomatoes, remaining herbs and oil and cook for at least an hour to finish.

• Or make the entire dish ahead. It is best to make your ratatouille one or two days before serving so the flavors have a chance to meld and mellow. Once the dish is cooked and cooled, transfer it to a container, adding a little oil if necessary, and refrigerate for up to five days. When you're ready to serve, bring it to room temperature (this takes about an hour) and drizzle with a tiny bit more olive oil. You can also reheat it on the stove or in the microwave.

RATATOUILLE **65**

Choosing and Preparing the Vegetables

There are many ways you can cut the vegetables for ratatouille, but a combination of slices, rounds and spears gives the stew an attractive look and some textural contrast.

EGGPLANT is like the meat of the ratatouille, adding a savory heft and richness.

You can use any type of eggplant you like, though if the skin is tough and leathery, consider peeling it first. If you'd prefer to keep the skin on, which gives ratatouille a nice texture, look for tender, young, thin-skinned eggplant. In France, cooks often use large Italian purple-black eggplants. But you can also use graffiti, Japanese, Chinese or white eggplant varieties, or use a combination of them for the most interesting and diverse texture.

To prepare the eggplants, slice off the top and bottom from each. Lay an eggplant on its side and cut it in half, then cut it into 1-inch chunks or spears. Repeat with remaining eggplant.

PEPPERS give a jammy sweetness and fruitiness to the stew. Choose a combination of red, yellow and orange bell peppers, or other sweet peppers. Green bell peppers, which are harvested earlier than the red, orange and yellow ones, have a more pungent, grassy flavor and less sweetness; they are not what you want for ratatouille.

To prepare the peppers, lay one on its side and slice off the top and bottom. Halve the pepper, remove the seeds and cut out the white veins. Slice into ¼-inch-thick strips. Repeat with remaining peppers. Alternatively, after trimming and seeding the peppers, you can cut them into ¼-inch thick rounds.

66 THE NEW ESSENTIALS OF FRENCH COOKING

ZUCCHINI is soft, sweet and very succulent when slowly stewed in a ratatouille.

You can use any variety of zucchini you find—the fresher, the better. A mix of colors (yellow, dark green and pale green) makes for a particularly pretty dish. Always keep the skins on zucchini, or they will completely fall apart as they cook.

To prepare the zucchini, slice off the tops and bottoms. Lay each zucchini on its side. Cutting horizontally, slice into ¼-inch-thick rounds.

ONIONS add a caramelized sweetness to ratatouille.

Large Spanish onions or white onions (which have a high water content and some bite) are best here. Keep in mind that as the onions cook, they sweeten, so unless you want a particularly sweet ratatouille, avoid red onions, Vidalias and other high-sugar onions.

To prepare the onions, halve them from the stem to the root, then peel. Next, lay them flat. For ratatouille, aim for ¼-inch-thick slices—that is, unless you want more pronounced onion pieces in the dish, in which case you can cut thicker pieces. The thicker the slices, the longer the onions will take to roast.

Coq au Vin

coq·au·vin | kōk-o-van

Chicken braised in red wine with bacon, onions and mushrooms.

Why Master It?

Where would French cuisine be without wine?
It is as important in the pot as it is in the glass, the base
of myriad stews and braises. One of the best is coq au vin,
in which chicken is slowly simmered with red wine.

BRAISING CHICKEN IN WINE IS AN AGE-OLD TRADITION, and a method used all over France. You brown the meat, add liquid to the pot — be it water, wine or stock — and then set it over low heat for a lengthy simmer. That initial browning creates the foundation of the sauce, lending complex layers of flavor to the final dish.

In a traditional coq au vin, which hails from the Burgundy region, wine is used both to tenderize what was traditionally a tough old rooster (a coq in French) and to imbue the meat with its heady flavor. When the bird is slowly simmered, often for hours and hours as the oldest recipes suggest, its sinewy flesh slackens, growing soft and aromatic, and easily yielding to the fork. The wine, naturally, is a red Burgundy.

As the simmering wine seasons the chicken, the chicken seasons the wine, helping transform it into a savory sauce. The wine, which reduces as it cooks, also takes on the other flavors in the pot, in this case brandy, mushrooms, onions, bacon and herbs, along with the savory fond — the caramelized bits on the bottom of the pan that you get from the initial browning of the chicken. The young, tender chickens of today cook more quickly than those earlier birds, but they are imbued with similar lusty flavors.

For a dish that was supposed to use a tough, old bird, coq au vin has evolved into a more elegant dish, often found in good French restaurants around the world. While it's a great meal for a cold winter night, it's also scalable for a dinner party.

There are variations of coq au vin all over France, each a celebration of local wines both red and white. In Alsace, a dry riesling is used, resulting in a lighter, brighter sauce that is often enriched with a little cream or crème fraîche stirred in at the end. The Jura and the Champagne regions also have their own recipes; cooks in the Jura sometimes substitute morels for the more common white or brown button mushrooms, and using Champagne kicks up the elegance of the dish, especially with the addition of cream. In Beaujolais, the young dark purple nouveau wine gives that dish the name coq au violet. But Burgundy's version, made with its local wine, is the best known across France and all over the world.

No matter what kind of wine you pour into your pot, the method of simmering it with chicken or other meat is applicable across the kitchen. Case in point: Boeuf bourguignon, another French classic, is essentially coq au vin made with chunks of stewing beef instead of fowl. Mastering this one technique leads to many excellent dinners.

"Still Life" by Jacopo da Empoli (1551–1640).

A Brief History

LEGEND HAS IT THAT JULIUS CAESAR HIMSELF introduced a version of coq au vin to France. As the commonly cited (and thoroughly apocryphal) story goes, the Celtic Gauls sent a rooster to Caesar during the Roman occupation. Caesar had his cook stew it in herbs and Roman wine and then returned it to the Gauls. Whether or not this is true, the tradition of simmering poultry in wine does indeed date to ancient Rome, and perhaps even further back.

Because the main ingredient of a coq au vin was historically a tough old rooster, it is very likely that the earliest versions were peasant fare. Recipes calling for rooster rarely graced the early tracts on French cooking in the 17th and 18th centuries, which documented food for the wealthy. It wasn't until the more current substitution of tender chicken in the 19th century that the dish and all its variations entered the French canon.

That the Burgundian version emerged as the most prominent in the United States is because of Julia Child, who championed the recipe as a symbol of the sophistication and verve of French country cooking and frequently made it on her television program.

Coq au Vin

YIELD 4 SERVINGS | **TIME** 2½ HOURS, PLUS MARINATING

This recipe for coq au vin yields a supremely rich sauce filled with tender chicken, crisp bits of bacon, mushrooms and burnished pearl onions. Traditional versions call for a whole cut-up chicken, but using only dark meat gives you a particularly succulent dish. The crouton garnish adds a buttery crunch.

3 pounds chicken legs and thighs

2½ teaspoons kosher salt, more as needed

½ teaspoon freshly ground black pepper, more to taste

3 cups hearty red wine, preferably from Burgundy

1 bay leaf

1 teaspoon chopped fresh thyme leaves

4 ounces lardons, pancetta or bacon, diced into ¼-inch pieces (about 1 cup)

3 tablespoons extra-virgin olive oil, more as needed

1 large onion, diced

1 large carrot, peeled and diced

8 ounces white or brown mushrooms, halved if large, and sliced (about 4 cups)

(continued on page 76)

STEP 1 | Season chicken with 2¼ teaspoons salt and ½ teaspoon pepper. In a large bowl, combine chicken, wine, bay leaf and thyme. Cover and refrigerate for at least 2 hours or, even better, overnight.

STEP 2 | In a large Dutch oven or a heavy-bottomed pot with a tightfitting lid, cook lardons over medium-low heat until fat has rendered, and lardons are golden and crisp, 10 to 15 minutes. Using a slotted spoon, transfer lardons to a paper-towel-lined plate, leaving rendered fat in pot.

STEP 3 | Remove chicken from wine, reserving the marinade. Pat chicken pieces with paper towels until very dry. Heat lardon fat over medium heat until it's just about to smoke. Working in batches if necessary, add chicken in a single layer and cook until well browned, 3 to 5 minutes per side. (Add oil if the pot looks a little dry.) Transfer chicken to a plate as it browns.

STEP 4 | Add diced onion, carrot, half the mushrooms and the remaining ¼ teaspoon salt to pot. Cook until vegetables are lightly browned, about 8 minutes, stirring up any brown bits from the pot. Adjust heat if necessary to prevent burning.

COQ AU VIN **75**

Coq Au Vin | CONTINUED

2 garlic cloves, minced

1 teaspoon tomato paste

1 tablespoon all-purpose flour

2 tablespoons brandy

3 tablespoons unsalted butter

8 ounces peeled pearl onions
(about 12 to 15 onions)

Pinch sugar

2 slices white bread, cut into
triangles, crusts removed

¼ cup chopped parsley,
more for serving

STEP 5 | Stir in garlic and tomato paste and cook for 1 minute, then stir in flour and cook for another minute. Remove from heat, push vegetables to one side of pot, pour brandy into empty side, and ignite with a match. (If you're too nervous to ignite it, just cook brandy down for 1 minute.) Once the flame dies down, add reserved marinade, bring to a boil, and reduce halfway (to 1½ cups), about 12 minutes. Skim off any large pockets of foam that form on the surface.

STEP 6 | Add chicken, any accumulated juices and half the cooked lardons to the pot. Cover and simmer over low heat for 1 hour, turning halfway through. Uncover pot and simmer for 15 minutes to thicken. Taste and add salt and pepper, if necessary.

STEP 7 | Meanwhile, melt 1 tablespoon butter and 2 tablespoons oil in a nonstick or other large skillet over medium-high heat. Add pearl onions, a pinch of sugar and salt to taste. Cover, reduce heat to low and cook for 15 minutes, shaking skillet often to move onions around. Uncover. Push onions to one side of skillet, add remaining mushrooms, and raise heat to medium-high. Continue to cook until browned, stirring mushrooms frequently, and gently tossing onions occasionally, 5 to 8 minutes. Remove onions and mushrooms from skillet, and wipe it out.

STEP 8 | In same skillet, melt 2 tablespoons butter and 1 tablespoon oil over medium heat until bubbling. Add bread and toast on all sides until golden, about 2 minutes per side. (Adjust heat if needed to prevent burning.) Remove from skillet and sprinkle with salt.

STEP 9 | To serve, dip croutons in wine sauce, then coat in parsley. Add pearl onions, mushrooms and remaining half of the cooked lardons to the pot. Baste with wine sauce, sprinkle with parsley and serve with croutons on top.

Equipment You'll Need

Because you'll be cooking the dish for a long time and igniting brandy in it, a solidly built pot is a must.

DUTCH OVEN A 6- to 8-quart Dutch oven or heavy-bottomed pot with lid (a rondeau pot) is an essential tool for a braise. If the pot is too small, the liquid won't evaporate enough to give you a rich sauce; if it's too large, the wine in the pot won't sufficiently cover the chicken.

SKILLET The pearl onions and mushrooms for the topping are cooked separately from the chicken, so they have their own distinct flavor and texture. A 10-inch skillet with a lid is ideal.

TONGS A good pair of kitchen tongs will help you maneuver the chicken as you brown it, allowing you to fully sear the skin all over.

Techniques and Tips

You want to build flavor in the pan at every step, which enriches the sauce and gives it body. That begins with the meat, which should be seared deeply.

PREPARING AND BROWNING THE CHICKEN

• Using only bone-in dark meat makes the stew richer and thicker, because of the marrow in the bones. And dark meat isn't as prone to drying out as white meat. However, it is traditional to use a whole chicken, cut into pieces, and you can do that if you'd prefer; just add the breast to the pot 30 minutes after adding the dark meat.

• Marinating the chicken before browning it will give you a more evenly seasoned bird whose flesh is fully imbued with wine. The ideal marination time is 24 hours, but even four to six hours helps the cause.

NOTES

- For a good sear, the chicken must be fully dry, or moisture will steam the skin instead of browning it. Pat it well with paper towels after marinating.

- Take your time when browning the meat; it's one of the most important steps for getting robust flavor out of the chicken, and creates a brawny base for the sauce. Plan to spend at least 15 to 25 minutes at the stove for this step, searing the pieces in batches. Use tongs to hold the chicken and change its position, pressing it into the pan when necessary, so that all sides make contact with the hot metal to get a deep sear.

COOKING AND SERVING

- Some coq au vin recipes call for chicken stock to replace a portion of the wine, which accentuates meaty notes in the finished sauce. But this can dilute the wine flavor. The bacon and the searing of the chicken skin provide sufficient meatiness here, so this recipe omits the stock.

- Sautéing the tomato paste with the vegetables caramelizes the tomato. It also eliminates any metallic flavor from canned tomato paste.

- Adding flour to the pot helps thicken the sauce. Here, it is stirred into the vegetables while they're browning, which allows the taste of raw flour to cook off.

COQ AU VIN 79

NOTES

• Brandy brings complexity to the final dish. Igniting the brandy in the pot is a quick way to cook out much of the alcohol, and it's easier than you think. Use a long-handled igniter or match to light the flame. It burns out pretty quickly, so there is not much to fear. However, you can skip this step and simply let the brandy cook down in the pan for 1 minute.

• Here, the wine is boiled down for about 12 minutes before the chicken is added to the pot. Intensifying the sauce without overcooking the chicken.

• One quick way to peel pearl onions for the topping is to blanch them for 1 minute in a pot of boiling water. Drain, let cool, then slip off their skins. (Frozen peeled onions tend to be very soggy, and therefore much harder to caramelize because of their high moisture content. Use them only as a last resort.)

• A garnish of crisp toasted bread provides a textural contrast to the soft chicken, but feel free to leave it out.

• Like all braises, coq au vin is best made a day ahead, so the flavors can intensify. Let it cool completely, then store it in the refrigerator. To reheat, spoon off and discard any solidified fat, then heat over a low flame for about 20 to 30 minutes, stirring occasionally. Or reheat it in a 350-degree oven for about 30 minutes. Prepare the onions and mushrooms, and the croutons, just before serving.

• Serve with a green salad, and a good bottle of Burgundy.

Variation: Beef Bourguignon

YIELD 4 TO 6 SERVINGS | **TIME** 2½ HOURS, PLUS MARINATING

Like coq au vin, its sister dish from Burgundy, boeuf Bourguignon is a stew of meat slowly simmered in red wine along with pearl onions, mushrooms and bacon. Use a good wine here, something simple but drinkable. It makes all the difference in the finished dish. As with all beef stews, this one is best made a day or two ahead, but don't sauté the mushrooms and onions until just before serving.

3 pounds beef chuck or other boneless stewing beef, cut into 2-inch cubes and patted dry

2¼ teaspoons kosher salt, more to taste

½ teaspoon freshly ground black pepper

5 ounces lardons, pancetta or bacon, diced (about 1 ¼ cups)

1 onion, finely chopped

1 large carrot, sliced

2 garlic cloves, minced

1 teaspoon tomato paste

2 tablespoons all-purpose flour

1 750-milliliter bottle of red wine

1 large bay leaf

(continued on page 82)

STEP 1 | Season beef with 2 teaspoons salt and ½ teaspoon pepper. Set aside for at least 30 minutes at room temperature, or chill in the refrigerator for up to 24 hours.

STEP 2 | In a large Dutch oven or heavy-bottomed pot with a tightfitting lid, cook lardons over medium-low heat until fat is rendered and lardons are browned and crisp, about 10 to 15 minutes. Transfer with a slotted spoon to a paper towel-lined plate. Reserve fat in pot.

STEP 3 | Heat oven to 350 degrees. Raise heat under pot to medium-high and cook until fat is starting to smoke. Lay half the beef cubes in a single layer in the pot, leaving space between pieces. Cook until well browned on all sides, 10 to 15 minutes; transfer pieces to a plate as they brown. Repeat with remaining beef.

STEP 4 | Reduce heat, if necessary, to prevent burning. Stir in onion, carrot and remaining ¼ teaspoon salt and cook until soft, about 10 minutes, stirring occasionally.

STEP 5 | Stir in garlic and tomato paste, and cook for 1 minute. Stir in flour, cook for 1 minute, then add wine, bay leaf

COQ AU VIN **81**

Beef Bourguignon | CONTINUED

1 large sprig of thyme

8 ounces pearl onions, peeled
(about 12 to 15 onions)

8 ounces cremini mushrooms,
halved if large (about 4 cups)

1 tablespoon extra-virgin
olive oil

Pinch sugar

Chopped flat-leaf parsley,
for garnish

and thyme, scraping up brown bits at bottom of pot. Add browned beef and half the cooked lardons back to pot, cover, and transfer to oven. Let cook until beef is very tender, about 1½ hours, turning meat halfway through.

STEP 6 | Meanwhile, in a large skillet set over high heat, combine pearl onions, mushrooms, ¼ cup water, the olive oil and a pinch each of salt, pepper and sugar. Bring to a simmer, then cover and reduce heat to medium, cooking for 15 minutes. Uncover, raise heat to high and cook, tossing frequently, until vegetables are well browned, 5 to 7 minutes.

STEP 7 | To serve, scatter onions and mushrooms and remaining cooked lardons over stew, then top with parsley.

Steak

Beef seared in a hot skillet and
served with a red wine pan sauce.

Why Master It?

A ruby-rare steak napped with buttery sauce is
classic bistro fare, be it steak frites with a sharp
béarnaise, entrecôte au poivre with a peppery bite
or a simple rib steak with a red wine reduction.

THERE ARE FEW FASTER, easier and more impressive paths to dinner than to sauté a juicy steak
over a hot flame, then whisk together a sauce from the coppery drippings in the pan.

Although the technique for making pan sauce is used here with beef, it is easily adaptable
to all sorts of meats, including pork, lamb, chicken, veal and even fish.

A proper pan sauce begins with browning the meat. The pan needs to be hot enough to
sear the meat and cause a Maillard reaction, the caramelizing of amino acids and sugars.

After the meat is cooked to taste, it is removed from the pan, leaving behind a seared-on
layer of browned bits called the fond. This culinary gold contains an incredible savory character
that forms the foundation of the sauce. To access that meaty flavor, the fond must be dissolved
into a liquid; this is called deglazing the pan. Any liquid can be used, and water and stock
frequently are. But something alcoholic and acidic, like wine, is better at extracting the flavors.

A classic method of building a pan sauce, which we use here, is to develop the flavors in
stages. First, brandy is used to deglaze the pan, then wine and stock are added and simmered
down until syrupy. At the very end, butter is whisked into the pan to thicken the sauce, giving
it a silky texture that helps it cling to the steak for serving. Other liquids can stand in for the
brandy, wine and stock: fruit and vegetable juices, cream or milk, condiments like soy sauce
and chile paste, vinegars and spirits.

Once you've learned this adaptable technique, you will always be able to whisk up a fast
and pungent pan sauce from whatever fond your pan has produced.

STEAK **87**

A Brief History

SINCE THE EARLIEST BOVINES MET THE SPEARS OF OUR ANCESTORS, steaks have been prepared pretty much the same way. The cuts were grilled over a fire to quickly sear what many consider to be the choicest, most tender part of the animal. (By contrast, think of the stewing, braising and roasting necessary for larger and tougher cuts.)

Innovations in pans and the creation of the modern stove have changed things slightly, but the goal is the same, which is to brown the outside of the meat while preserving the juiciness of the middle. This can be done on green wooden sticks or hot rocks, over a grill, or in a metal or earthenware pan, over wood, charcoal, gas or electricity.

But the sauce accompanying steak has had a more varied history. And it's one that exemplifies the evolution of French cuisine over the centuries.

The earliest European sauces, which date to ancient times, were distinct from the meat, fish or vegetables with which they were served, prepared separately and from their own set of ingredients. The reasons were medicinal, rather than for the sake of taste. Based on the theory of humorism, a sauce was meant to balance out the intrinsic qualities of other ingredients in the dish to create a harmonious and health-giving meal. Pork, which was considered to be inherently moist and cold, might be paired with spicy, acidic sauces, to counter any potential upset of humors in the person eating it.

By the 17th century, a new French cuisine had begun to emerge. The focus shifted to enhancing the natural taste of foods rather than smothering them in spices and vinegars for purported health benefits. The ancestors of modern French sauces can be found in cookbooks from that era, in which herbs replaced spices, wine and stock eased the reliance on vinegar and verjus, and flour and butter roux, rather than bread crumbs, were used as thickeners. The practice of deglazing a pan to make the base for an elaborate sauce grew in popularity.

Over time sauces became richer and more voluptuous, beaten with butter, eggs and flour to achieve a thick and satiny consistency. In the 1830s, Marie-Antoine Carême first wrote about four mother sauces: espagnole (a demi-glace-based brown sauce), velouté (a stock-based sauce thickened with roux), béchamel (a creamy milk-based sauce) and allemande (a velouté thickened with eggs and cream). Auguste Escoffier would later refine Carême's classification, demoting allemande to a subset of velouté (despite the eggs and cream) and adding tomato sauce and hollandaise to the list.

These mother sauces remained central in French kitchens until the birth of the nouvelle cuisine movement of the 1960s. As the country's top chefs worked to simplify the national cuisine, they moved away from heavy sauces. (One of the 10 commandments for the movement, laid out in a 1973 article by the pioneering restaurant critics Henri Gault and Christian Millau, "Vive la Nouvelle Cuisine Francaise": "You will eliminate rich sauces.") Rather than relying on roux as thickeners, French chefs turned to the lighter touch of lemon juice, butter and herbs.

That approach lives on. Instead of deglazing a pan to use the resulting liquid in an intricate sauce, cooks now savor the mixture as a simple yet elegant sauce in its own right.

Pan-Seared Steak With Red Wine Sauce

YIELD 4 SERVINGS | **TIME** 35 MINUTES

You can use any cut of steak, either bone-in or boneless, to make this classic French bistro dish. Open a good bottle of red wine for the pan sauce, preferably one that you're happy to finish off with dinner.

Kosher salt, as needed

Freshly ground black pepper, as needed

1½ pounds boneless steak, or 1¾ pounds bone-in steak (1½ inches thick)

2 shallots

2½ tablespoons unsalted butter

½ teaspoon neutral oil, such as grapeseed

2 tablespoons good brandy, preferably Cognac

⅓ cup dry red wine

⅓ cup beef or chicken stock, preferably homemade

1 tablespoon chopped chives

Watercress, for serving

STEP 1 | Generously sprinkle salt and pepper all over steaks, then let steaks rest uncovered for 15 minutes at room temperature. Meanwhile, mince the shallots.

STEP 2 | Melt ½ tablespoon butter and the oil in a large skillet over medium-high heat until almost smoking. Add steaks and cook until done to taste, about 3 to 4 minutes per side for rare and a little longer for medium-rare or medium. (Bone-in steaks take a few minutes longer to cook through than boneless.) If the pan begins to smoke or burn, lower the heat Transfer steaks to a plate to rest while you prepare the sauce.

STEP 3 | Add shallots to the skillet and cook over medium heat until lightly browned, about 1 minute. Add brandy to the skillet and use a long-handled match or igniter to set the brandy on fire. (Stand back when you do this.) Let flames die out, then add red wine and cook until reduced and syrupy, 2 to 4 minutes. Add stock and boil until reduced and thickened, 3 to 4 minutes longer.

STEP 4 | Remove pan from heat and whisk in remaining tablespoons butter and the chives. Serve steaks and sauce immediately with watercress.

Equipment You'll Need

A good steak deserves a good pan, especially if you're setting brandy on fire. A meat thermometer is a must.

STAINLESS STEEL PAN These are best for cooking pan sauces with a good dose of acidity; enamel-lined pans also work well. Carbon steel and cast iron pans are reactive and could discolor the sauce, though this isn't a deal breaker, so if that is all you've got, use it. But do avoid nonstick pans. Your drippings, upon which the sauce is built, won't brown nearly as well.

MEAT THERMOMETER It is worthwhile to learn how to test your steak for doneness with your fingers, but it also helps to have a good meat thermometor. Digital thermometers will give you a more exact reading, and they usually work very quickly. Test at the thickest part of the meat, away from bone.

Techniques and Tips

There's more to searing a steak than a hot pan and a good piece of meat, though that is the right place to start. And learning how to use the drippings for a fast pan sauce will help you make the most out of every meal, whether you're cooking steaks, chops, fish or chicken.

CHOOSING AND COOKING THE STEAK

The French butcher the cow differently from the English and Americans. They divide tough and tender meats, creating high-quality cuts like fillets from the sirloin region (chateaubriand being the thickest, then tournedos, faux filet and filet mignon) and entrecôte from the fore rib region. One of the most desired French cuts is the onglet (hanger steak), cut just below the sirloin region.

NOTES

This said, you can use any good steak in this recipe, either a boneless or bone-in cut. Boneless cuts take less time to cook, so start checking them for doneness before you'd check bone-in meat. Filet mignon, cut from the tenderloin, will give you the softest and most tender meat, but has less fat (and less flavor) than other cuts. Rib-eye and other sirloin cuts are a little chewier, but have a deeper, beefier flavor. You could also use a thinner steak (hanger, strip, flank), but watch them closely so they don't overcook.

• You need some fat on your steak. Look for marbling. Fat equals flavor, both for the meat itself and also for the pan sauce.

• Seasoning the steak at least 15 minutes before cooking (and up to 24 hours if you keep it in the refrigerator) gives the meat time to absorb the salt evenly. If you season it several hours in advance, you can press herbs and-or minced garlic all over the surface of the steak, then wipe it off just before cooking so nothing burns.

• Cooking steak in butter gives the meat excellent flavor. But since butter can burn, it is often combined with a little grapeseed oil, which raises its smoking point. Or you can use all oil if you prefer. Clarified butter and ghee also work well.

• For optimal browning, which results in a flavorful pan sauce, get your skillet very hot before adding the meat, letting it heat for at least 3 to 5 minutes. A drop of water should immediately sizzle when flicked into the pan.

NOTES

- The timing of your steak depends on the skillet, your stove and the temperature of the meat when it hits the pan. For rare steak, cook to 120 degrees; medium-rare is 130. Learn how meat cooked to those temperatures feels when you tap it with your fingers, and then use that to guide you in the future. For medium-rare, the meat should offer some resistance but not feel firm, which indicates a well-done steak. Rare meat is a bit softer.

- Rest your steaks before slicing them. Put the meat on a cutting board and tent with foil. Let it sit for 5 to 10 minutes. This helps the meat reabsorb the juices and will also raise the temperature slightly. Do this every time you cook steak; it's always a good idea to keep those juices.

- You must cook the steaks and the sauce in immediate succession, and just before serving. Once you start, there isn't much waiting around. If you're making this for a dinner party, don't start cooking until all your guests arrive.

NOTES

MAKING THE SAUCE

- The alcohol in wine and brandy helps dissolve and release the pan drippings, extracting their flavor. While you can also deglaze a pan with stock or water, it won't be as intensely flavorful. Much of the alcohol cooks off.

- To quickly cook off much of the alcohol in the brandy, light it with a long match or igniter. Just make sure to step back before you do. The flame should die down in a few seconds. If you really don't want to set the alcohol on fire, you can simmer it down for a few minutes instead.

- Letting the liquids in your pan simmer until they are thick and syrupy is central to getting a silky sauce. Be sure to let them reduce before whisking in the butter and any herbs.

- If at any point your sauce separates and you can't seem to whisk it together into a smooth, emulsified liquid, scrape it into a blender and whirl it for a few seconds. That should fix it.

Béarnaise Sauce

Like hollandaise sauce, one of the mother sauces of French cuisine, Béarnaise is based on an emulsion of butter and egg yolks. It is seasoned with vinegar, tarragon and shallots for a savory edge.

¾ cup cold unsalted butter (1½ sticks) plus 2 tablespoons

3 tablespoons white-wine vinegar

¼ cup dry white wine or dry white vermouth

1 tablespoon shallots, minced

1 tablespoon minced fresh tarragon or chives

⅛ teaspoon black pepper

Pinch salt

3 egg yolks

2 tablespoons fresh parsley, minced

STEP 1 | Melt 1½ sticks unsalted butter; set aside. In a heavy-bottomed, nonreactive skillet, combine white-wine vinegar, dry white wine or vermouth, shallots, tarragon or chives, pepper and salt. Simmer until the liquid has reduced to 2 tablespoons. Let cool.

STEP 2 | Beat egg yolks until thick and sticky, about 1 minute. Strain the vinegar mixture into the yolks, and beat until combined. Add 1 tablespoon of cold butter, but do not beat it in.

STEP 3 | Scrape egg mixture back into skillet, and place over very low heat. Stir with a wire whisk until yolks slowly thicken, about 1 to 2 minutes. Beat in another tablespoon of cold butter, then beat in melted butter in a slow, steady stream until sauce thickens, its consistency should be like mayonnaise. (You may not need all the butter.) Taste and correct seasoning, then beat in minced parsley.

STEP 4 | Serve the sauce warm, not hot. It will keep for up to 5 days in the fridge.

Horseradish Crème Fraîche Sauce

Easily made in less than 5 minutes, this piquant, creamy sauce can be stirred together a few days in advance and gets even better as it sits (which it can do for up to 3 days).

1 cup crème fraîche

2 tablespoons white horseradish

1 tablespoon chives, minced

1 teaspoon mustard

Kosher salt and freshly ground black pepper

STEP 1 | In a small bowl, whisk together ingredients; add salt and pepper to taste.

Herbed Compound Butter

A decadently rich combination of butter, garlic and herbs, a small slice of compound butter goes a long way on a steak. And leftovers freeze perfectly for up to six months.

½ cup unsalted butter (1 stick), softened

1 tablespoon shallots, minced or 1 garlic clove, minced

1 tablespoon fresh thyme or rosemary, chopped

1 teaspoon fresh lemon juice

¼ teaspoon black pepper

¼ teaspoon fine sea salt

STEP 1 | In a bowl, mash together all ingredients.

STEP 2 | Spoon the butter onto a piece of parchment paper or plastic wrap, form into a log and wrap well.

STEP 3 | Chill for at least 3 hours before using.

STEAK **97**

Tagine

ta·gine | tä'zhēn

A North African stew made with a mix
of spiced meat, vegetables and fruit.

Why Master It?

Revered for its balance of sweet and savory flavors, the tagine journeyed from North Africa to France, a link to the country's colonial past. The fragrant stew gradually found its way into home kitchens.

TAGINE ISN'T PART OF THE CODIFIED FRENCH CUISINE, nor is it something you'll find at traditional French restaurants, either in France or abroad.

But given the estimated five million people of North African descent in France, and the excellence of the dish—soft chunks of meat, vegetables or both, deeply scented with spices and often lightly sweetened with fruit—it is no surprise that tagine has taken hold.

The dish is very similar to a French ragout, a slowly simmered stew of meat and vegetables. But while a ragoût nearly always calls for a significant amount of wine (and often broth), to help braise the meat, a tagine needs little additional liquid because of the pot—also called a tagine—used to prepare the dish. With its tightfitting, cone-shaped lid, a tagine steams the stew as it cooks, catching the rising, aromatic vapor and allowing it to drip back over the ingredients. (A Dutch oven with a tightfitting lid will accomplish nearly the same thing.)

The intensity of the spicing also sets the tagine apart from a ragoût, which tends to use aromatics rather than ground spices for flavor. But a heady mix of spices, called ras el hanout, is at the heart of a good tagine. In North Africa, each cook traditionally makes a highly complex spice blend. In our recipe, we use a simple mixture of spices that are easy to find.

A tagine usually strives for a balance of sweet and savory. Spices like ginger, cinnamon or clove bring out the sweetness of the meat, alongside braised fruit (apricots, prunes or raisins) and savory seasonings (parsley, pepper or saffron). The dish is usually served with flatbread for dipping in the complex and fragrant sauce.

A Brief History

THE TAGINE IS A MOROCCAN DISH, though It Is common throughout the North African region known as the Maghreb, which also includes Algeria and Tunisia. The earliest versions, recorded in the 10th century, represent the intersection of two cultures, those of the native Berbers and of the Muslim Arabs of the conquest. When the spices of the Middle East met the stews of the indigenous Berber cuisine, the tagine was born.

Those spices and tastes had entered Middle Eastern cuisine with the spread of Islam across the broader region, which absorbed the flavors of its expanding territories. In the seventh century, as the capital of the Muslim caliphate moved from Mecca to Damascus, Muslims met Greeks and Romans, Egyptians, Persians and Franks across the Arabian desert. Cinnamon and cardamom were added to the pantry.

In the eighth century, the capital moved again, this time to Baghdad, and by the ninth century, the cuisine had become saturated with spices and full of elaborate and highly embellished dishes. It was common among the wealthy to use at least two dozen different spices and half a dozen herbs in one dish, not to mention dried fruit, nuts, honey, flowers and perfumed essences, like orange blossom water.

Those ingredients gradually found their way to the Maghreb, heavily influencing the local cuisine, including what would become the tagine. Although contemporary North African cooking is somewhat stripped down from its ornate past, many of those perfumed, spiced and honeyed flavors remain. Tunisian tangines usually use a lamb or veal shank.

Food from the Maghreb first surfaced in France after it conquered Algeria in 1830 and later annexed Tunisia and Morocco. French domination of the region lasted until 1955, when Morocco gained independence, followed by Tunisia in 1956 and Algeria in 1962.

The cuisine truly gained a foothold in France during the immigration surge of the 1970s, when the French government admitted large numbers of North Africans, who settled in subsidized housing in banlieues (suburbs). Restaurants serving tagines and couscous started popping up in and around large cities in France, particularly Paris and Marseille. And the spicy lamb sausages called merguez were turned into a street food snack, stuffed into a baguette and topped with French fries (known as merguez frites).

As the French developed a taste for North African food (which is called cuisine Maghrébin), chefs and cookbook authors began translating the recipes, and cooks flocked to the kitchen.

Lamb Tagine

YIELD 8 SERVINGS | **TIME** 4 HOURS

Although you can make tagine with any meat, fish or vegetable, lamb adds heady flavor to this complex stew. Here, dried apricots, cinnamon, nutmeg and almonds provide sweetness, while saffron, turmeric, tomato paste and herbs make it deeply savory. The result is a stunning centerpiece of a dish, one that begs to be piled onto your most beautiful platter before serving.

3 pounds bone-in lamb stew meat or lamb neck, cut into 1½-inch pieces

2½ teaspoons kosher salt, more as needed

1¾ cups lamb or chicken stock

5 ounces (1 cup) dried apricots

2 tablespoons extra-virgin olive oil, more as needed

2 large onions, thinly sliced

1 teaspoon tomato paste

½ teaspoon grated fresh ginger

2 small cinnamon sticks

Large pinch saffron

½ teaspoon ground ginger

¾ teaspoon ground turmeric

(continued on page 106)

STEP 1 | In a large bowl, combine lamb and 2 teaspoons salt. Let sit at room temperature at least 1 hour or up to 24 hours in the refrigerator.

STEP 2 | In a small pot, bring stock to a boil. Remove from heat, add apricots, and let sit at least 15 minutes.

STEP 3 | Heat oven to 325 degrees. In a tagine, Dutch oven or heavy-bottomed pot with a tightfitting lid, warm 2 tablespoons oil over medium heat until hot. Working in batches, add lamb to pot, leaving room around each piece (this will help them brown). Cook until well browned on all sides, about 10 minutes. Transfer pieces to a plate as they brown.

STEP 4 | Drain fat, if necessary, leaving just enough to coat the bottom of the pot. Add onions and ¼ teaspoon salt, and cook until soft, about 8 minutes. Add tomato paste, ginger, 1 cinnamon stick and the spices, and cook until fragrant, about 2 minutes. Add lamb and any juices on the plate, the apricots and stock, and half the cilantro. Cover pot with foil and then its lid, and cook in oven for 2½ to 3 hours, or until lamb is tender, turning it occasionally. (If using a tagine, you don't need to use foil.) Taste and adjust seasonings, if necessary.

TAGINE **105**

Lamb Tagine | CONTINUED

¾ teaspoon ground
black pepper

¼ teaspoon ground cinnamon

Pinch freshly grated nutmeg

⅓ cup fresh cilantro, chopped

1 tablespoon unsalted butter

½ cup slivered almonds

2 scallions, finely chopped

1 tablespoons chopped
parsley

Fresh lemon juice, to taste

STEP 5 | Meanwhile, in a small skillet, heat butter and 1 cinnamon stick over medium heat. Add almonds and ¼ teaspoon salt, and cook until golden brown, 5 to 7 minutes. Discard cinnamon stick.

STEP 6 | To serve, transfer lamb and juices to a serving platter. Top with toasted almonds and any butter left in the small skillet, scallions, parsley and remaining cilantro. Sprinkle with fresh lemon juice to taste. Serve with flat bread or couscous, if desired.

Equipment You'll Need

Though most pots will do, tagines are beautiful clay or ceramic vessels that can also decorate your kitchen.

TAGINE OR DUTCH OVEN A tagine is the traditional clay cooking vessel for the dish; it has a base that is wider than it is tall, cone-shape top. But you don't need a tagine to make this recipe. Use a Dutch oven or another lidded pot instead, as long as the lid fits tightly. If it doesn't, cover the pot with foil before placing the lid on top to seal in the juice.

TONGS A tagine, like most braises, starts with the browning of the meat. A good pair of tongs will help you maneuver the lamb as you sear it in the pot.

SMALL SKILLET Sliced almonds, which are used in the topping, will toast quickly and evenly in a small skillet. Choose a heavy-duty one so you won't get a hot spot, which could burn the nuts.

Techniques and Tips

The gorgeous aromas and flavors of a tagine are what set it apart from all other stews. Choose and use your spices with care, and take time to fully brown the meat.

BUYING SPICES AND BUILDING FLAVOR IN THE POT

• Fresh spices are integral to getting an intensely flavored sauce. To tell if your spices are fresh, smell them. Empty a bit into the palm of your hand; if it isn't noticeably fragrant, then it won't add noticeable flavor to the tagine. If you have only stale spices, add a little more than what the recipe calls for.

• It is often more economical to shop at a spice retailer. They tend to grind the spices more frequently on site, which means that they are not only fresher when you buy them, they will also last longer in your pantry.

TAGINE **107**

NOTES

- Some recipes use ras el hanout, a North African spice mix that contains black pepper, cardamom, cinnamon, clove, coriander, cumin, mace, paprika and turmeric, among other spices. Each mix is different and contains up to 30 different spices. Here, we make our own simplified version. Do not substitute another ras el hanout blend for our mixture; each blend is unique and can be quite different, so it may not work well in this recipe. (Most Moroccan cookbooks give their own instructions for ras el hanout, and then tailor their recipes to it.) Toasting the spices adds yet another layer of flavor.

- Both ground cinnamon and cinnamon sticks are used in our recipe. They have slightly different flavors and work together for a more nuanced cinnamon taste in both the meat and the sauce.

- The contrast of sweet and savory is a hallmark of North African cuisine. Tagine recipes commonly include some kind of dried fruit to supply that sweetness. Here, we use apricots, which are tart as well as sweet. Raisins, prunes and dates are other options.

- Taking a moment to cook the tomato paste in oil before adding liquid caramelizes the paste, enriching its flavor. It also rids the tomato paste of any metallic taste, which can be a problem with canned paste.

- Adding half the herbs at the beginning of cooking and half at the end gives the tagine both depth of flavor and a pop of freshness.

- Personalize this recipe to suit your tastes. Use bone-in beef instead of lamb for a less gamy and slightly sweeter flavor. (Beef can have more fat, so make the tagine a day ahead, chill it, then remove excess fat from the surface.) Swap raisins, prunes or dates for the apricots. Chunks or slices of winter squash lend a delicate, velvety sweetness; add them during the last 45 minutes of cooking, along with a few tablespoons of water if the pot looks dry.

NOTES

PREPARING THE LAMB

- Bone-in lamb gives this tagine a rich sauce, thanks to the marrow content of the bones, along with plenty of soft, succulent meat. Lamb neck, if you can get it, is particularly juicy.

- Salting the lamb ahead of time helps the seasoning penetrate the meat, flavoring it thoroughly. While even an hour makes a difference, if you have time, you can salt the meat up to 24 hours ahead.

- Browning the meat gives the sauce a deeper flavor. Take your time doing this. Let each piece brown fully on all sides, and use tongs to hold up the meat if necessary, to brown the irregularly shaped pieces.

NOTES

SERVING THE TAGINE

• Tagines are generally served with flatbread for dipping in all the lovely sauce. You can use any type of flatbread—pita bread works nicely—served either at room temperature or warmed up so it is pliable. If you warm the bread, keep it wrapped in a clean cloth so it retains the heat.

• You can also serve your tagine with couscous, either on the side or spread in a shallow platter with the tagine poured on top. Polenta is another good, though unorthodox, option.

Variations

There are countless tagine variations, with cooks personalizing the recipe to suit their tastes. Feel free to come up with your own combinations. Just be sure to keep it sweet and savory.

MEAT Use beef instead of lamb for a less gamy and slightly sweeter flavor. Choose bone-in cuts such as shanks or short ribs. Beef can have a higher fat content than lamb, so if you do make the substitution, cook the tagine the day before serving, then scoop off the fat from the surface before reheating.

FRUIT You can use any dried fruit here instead of apricots. Sweet jammy dates are a more intensely sugary substitute, and they are highly traditional. Golden raisins are a more tart option. Figs, prunes and dark raisins can also be used.

VEGETABLES Feel free to add vegetables to the tagine if you like. Chunks or slices of winter squash, either peeled or not, lend a delicate, velvety sweetness. Other options include eggplant, zucchini and tomatoes. Add them to the pot during the last 45 minutes of cooking, along with a few tablespoons of water if the pot looks dry when you put them in.

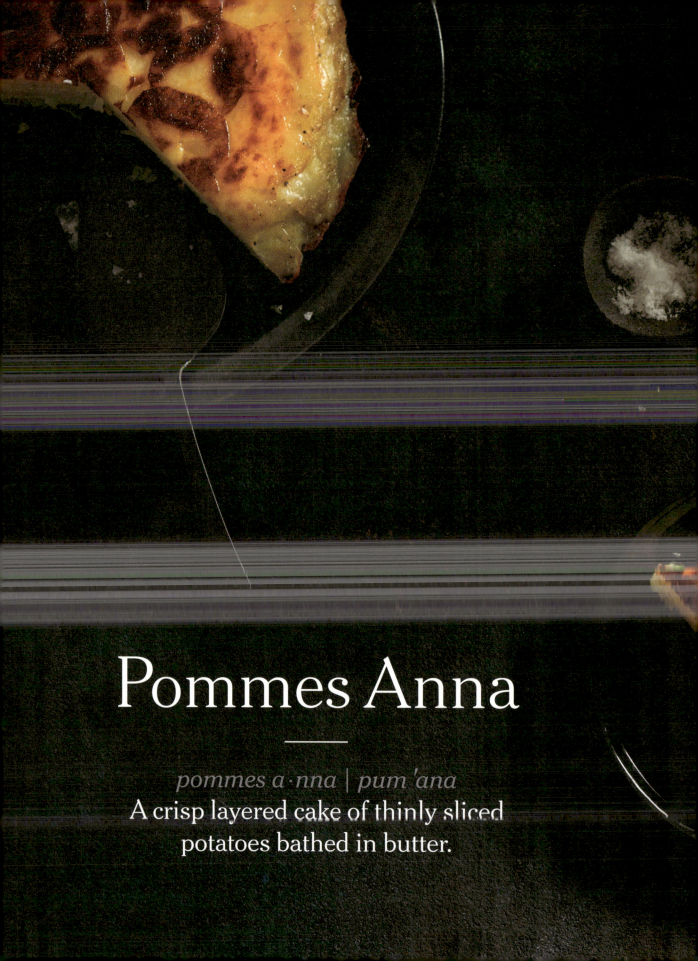

Pommes Anna

―

pommes a·nna | pum ˈana
A crisp layered cake of thinly sliced
potatoes bathed in butter.

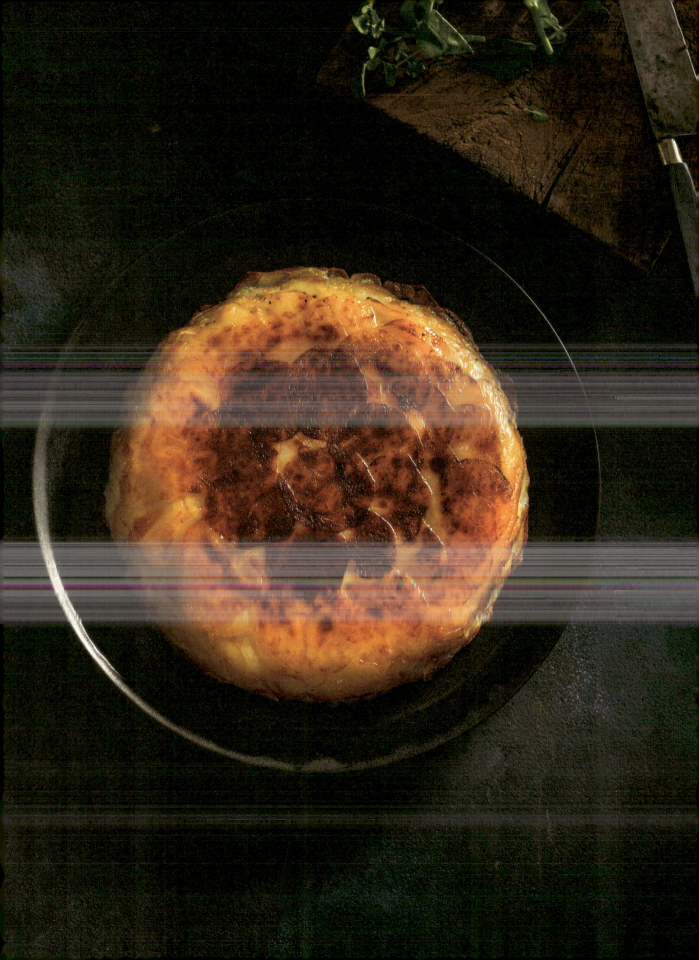

Why Master It?

With only two main ingredients, butter and potatoes, pommes Anna is a minimalist triumph of French technique. It is also one of the more challenging potato dishes to prepare and a true glory to any cook who makes it correctly.

CRISP FRITES, CREAMY GRATINS—the French do beautiful things with potatoes. And of all the magnificent potato dishes the French make with pommes de terre, pommes Anna is a classic and simple dish, one that deserves more acclaim beyond France.

A buttery cake composed of paper-thin slices of potato, pommes Anna is similar to potato gratin in the way it is layered and baked. But unlike a gratin, which is lightly browned on top and creamy soft all the way through, pommes Anna emerges from the oven with a tender, slippery interior and a crunchy golden crust. It is a gorgeous contrast in textures.

To make it, the potatoes are trimmed into cylinders (to ensure a neat and attractive shape), sliced and then layered into a skillet sizzling with clarified butter. The potatoes are first cooked on top of the stove, to sear and brown them on the bottom, then moved to the oven to bake until the slices in the center turn soft. After baking, the pan is inverted onto a platter and presented as a stunning, burnished cake of crunchy potato petals.

You can dress up the basic recipe with an array of aromatics, cheeses and other vegetables. (Here, we've added an optional touch of garlic for a sweetly pungent contrast to the mild potatoes.) But pommes Anna doesn't need it. The simple flavor of potato and butter is always a comfort, but the interplay of crisp and soft in this dish elevates it to another plane.

"Peasants Harvesting Potatoes During the Flood of the Rhine in 1852" wby Gustave Brion.

A Brief History

POMMES ANNA WAS CREATED IN THE MID-19TH CENTURY by the chef Adolphe Duglére at Café Anglais in Paris. It was most likely named after Anna Deslions, one of the café's grandes cocottes, who is said to have entertained an international coterie of princes and other dignitaries in a private salon above the dining room.

It's telling that the dish was named for a glamorous courtesan. At that time, the potato still had a somewhat shady reputation among the French, having been considered poisonous for centuries after its introduction to Europe. It seemed delectable, yet just a little bit dangerous.

Potatoes arrived in France in the 16th century via the Spanish, who encountered them in what is now Colombia. The combination of the Northern French climate and the varieties of potato that were imported produced sad, watery tubers, thought to be toxic and unfit for human consumption. As late as 1748, potatoes were outlawed as crops in Paris. Because of their resemblance to the twisted limbs of lepers, the tubers were believed to cause the disease.

This began to change in the late 18th century because of Antoine-Augustin Parmentier, a French army officer who developed a taste for potatoes in a Prussian jail in Hamburg, where he was held captive after the Seven Years' War. Parmentier persuaded King Louis XVI to embrace the potato, both as a delicacy for the court when dressed up with cream and butter, and as cheap, reliable food for the poor when made into soups and gruels. His name is linked to several French potato dishes, including hachis Parmentier, a baked dish of minced meat and mashed potatoes, and potage Parmentier, a puréed leek and potato soup.

Over the next centuries, potato preparations flourished, and potatoes soon became a necessary accompaniment to roasts, stews and sautéed dishes across the French repertoire de cuisine. Today, pommes Anna is considered to be among the finest of all French potato dishes, one skillful cooks take pride in making.

Pommes Anna

YIELD 6 SERVINGS | **TIME** 1½ HOURS

This recipe brings out the best in the humble potato, with a crisp exterior and satiny slices within, all of them bathed in clarified butter. The garlic isn't traditional, but adds pungent sweetness. Serve it alongside roasted meat, or top it with eggs for an unusual main course.

5½ to 7 pounds russet or all-purpose white potatoes, as needed

¾ cup clarified butter, melted (recipe on page 50)

Fine sea salt, as needed

Freshly ground black pepper, as needed

2 to 4 garlic cloves, sliced paper-thin on a mandoline (optional)

STEP 1 | Heat oven to 450 degrees. Place a rack in the middle and set a rimmed baking sheet on top of it.

STEP 2 | Trim potatoes into cylinders, peeling any skin left after trimming. Using a mandoline or sharp knife, slice into ⅛-inch slices and blot dry with paper towels. You should have about 8½ cups.

STEP 3 | In a heavy 10-inch cast-iron skillet, heat 3 tablespoons clarified butter over medium heat. When hot, carefully place 1 potato slice in the middle, then quickly place more slices around it, overlapping them clockwise to make a ring. Place a second ring to surround the first, going counterclockwise. Continue to the edge of the pan, alternating the direction in which the potato rings overlap. Sprinkle with a generous ¼ teaspoon salt and pepper to taste, then drizzle with another 2 tablespoons butter.

STEP 4 | Create a second layer of potatoes, just as you did with the first. Dot a third of the garlic slices, if using, on top of this layer of potatoes. Season with salt and pepper; drizzle with some more butter.

STEP 5 | Continue layering potatoes, garlic, butter and salt until everything is used, making a dome of potatoes in the

POMMES ANNA **119**

Pommes Anna | CONTINUED

middle (they will sink as they cook). Occasionally shake skillet gently to ensure potatoes aren't sticking. When finished, there should be enough butter that it can be seen bubbling up the sides of the skillet.

STEP 6 | Butter the bottom of a 9-inch pan and one side of a piece of foil. Push the pan down firmly on top of the potatoes to press them. Remove pan, then cover potatoes with the foil, buttered side down. Cover the foil with a lid. Set skillet on the baking sheet in oven and bake for 20 minutes.

STEP 7 | Remove skillet from oven, uncover and remove foil, and again press potatoes down firmly with the 9-inch pan. (Rebutter bottom of pan, if necessary, before you press down.) Return to oven and bake uncovered, until potatoes are tender and the sides are dark brown when lifted away from skillet, 20 to 25 minutes.

STEP 8 | Once more, remove skillet from oven and press potatoes down firmly with pan. Tip the skillet away from you to drain off the excess butter into a bowl (this can be reused for cooking), using the lid to keep the potatoes in place. Run a thin spatula around edge and bottom of skillet to loosen any slices stuck to the pan. Carefully turn out the potatoes onto a serving platter.

Equipment You'll Need

A mandoline assures evenly sliced potatoes, but you can also practice your knife skills and do them by hand.

MANDOLINE This very sharp slicing tool allows you to cut potatoes thinly and evenly. There's no need to buy a pricey, stainless-steel model; an inexpensive plastic mandoline is fine and can go in the dishwasher. A sharp chef's knife will get the job done, but a mandoline is made for this task.

SKILLETS Traditionally, pommes Anna is cooked in a copper pan made specifically for that purpose. A skillet, either well-seasoned cast iron or heavy-duty nonstick, works just as well (or perhaps even better). Use one with a tightfitting cover. You'll also need a slightly smaller skillet or a saucepan for pressing down the potatoes, which helps compress the cake and cook it evenly.

RIMMED BAKING SHEET It's a good idea to place the skillet on a baking sheet in the oven; it promotes even browning of the potatoes and catches any sizzling butter overflow.

OFFSET SPATULA A small metal offset spatula, which has a long, thin, blunt blade (it is often used for frosting cakes), will help you remove the potatoes from the pan easily and in one piece. If you don't have one, use the smallest spatula you have, or a butter knife.

Techniques and Tips

What sets pommes Anna apart from other fried potato recipes is the refinement of its technique. All the tiny details, from the potatoes themselves to the way you slice them, may seem like a lot to absorb, but understanding them is essential to success.

CHOOSING INGREDIENTS

• For the potatoes, you can use either waxy boiling potatoes or starchy baking potatoes, depending on the texture you're after. Or, if you'd like, you can use a combination of the two.

I like Yukon Golds for this recipe, low-starch boiling potatoes, such as round white potatoes, red potatoes or Yukon golds. When you use these, the potato slices remain in distinct coins as opposed to merging into a uniform cake. These slippery potato pieces make it harder to cut through the cake neatly after unmolding. It can easily fall apart. But the buttery flavor and satiny texture of the waxy potatoes are marvelous, making up for the precarious presentation.

Russet baking potatoes make for a more compact cake; the starchy potato slices glue themselves into a uniform disk, one that slices into neat wedges. Texturally, the cake will have a crisp exterior with a mashed-potato-like heart. Because of their oblong shape, Russets are easier to work with than round potatoes, and you'll have less waste.

NOTES

- Use good butter: European-style butter with a high fat content (at least 82 percent) works best here because it contains less moisture than regular butter.

- You can make pommes Anna with unclarified butter, but it really is worth the few extra minutes it takes to make clarified butter first. It can take the heat for longer and at higher temperatures than butter that has not been clarified, so it will be less likely to burn.

- If you don't want to clarify your butter, use a combination of oil and regular butter instead. You will end up with a more neutral and less buttery flavor, but the recipe will still work. (If you decide not to clarify, then it is especially important to use that high-fat, European-style butter.) Or you could use ghee, which is basically clarified butter in which the milk solids have been allowed to brown before being removed. It has a lightly caramelized, nutty flavor.

TRIMMING THE POTATOES AND USING A MANDOLINE

- You need to trim the potatoes so they are about uniform in size, but don't obsess over it. Using a paring or chef's knife, remove the ends from each potato, then trim the sides so you end up with cylinders. It may seem like a lot of waste, especially if you are using round boiling potatoes, as opposed to oblong baking potatoes. Use the trimmings in mashed potatoes or soups.

- If you'd like, skip all the trimming and merely peel the potatoes. You won't get as nice a presentation when you unmold the cake, but if that doesn't bother you, you will save yourself a lot of work.

NOTES

• The beauty of a mandoline is that it gives you very thin and even slices of potato, and does so very quickly. (In this recipe, you are aiming for pieces that are ⅛-inch thick.) Take extreme care when using a mandoline. The blade is sharp, and your hand is moving quickly; it is easy to slice your finger. It's best to use the protective hand guard or gloves (the mesh gloves meant for shucking oysters work well).

• Once you have sliced the potatoes, it is essential to dry them so they don't stick to the pan. To do so, place the slices between paper towels on a counter and press slightly. Let them sit in the open air and dry, about 5 to 10 minutes. (One way to save time is to let them sit out while you clarify the butter.)

• Never rinse the potato slices. It removes their starch, which is what helps them bind together into a cake.

ASSEMBLING AND BAKING

• Before you begin layering the potatoes into the hot skillet, take a moment to place a baking sheet in the oven and preheat it. Later, you can place the skillet with the potatoes directly on the sheet, which will distribute the heat more evenly and catch any stray splashes of butter.

• Do not worry about forming a perfect circle of overlapping potatoes; it will look stunning even if a potato or two is not exactly aligned.

- Take care when adding the sliced potatoes to the hot butter. It can splatter and burn you. As long as you keep the pan at medium heat and add the slices quickly, you should be fine.

NOTES

- For a compact cake with uniform thickness, use a second skillet or large saucepan to press down on the potatoes. Choose one that is large enough to cover most of the potatoes, and butter the bottom of the pan. Press down on the potatoes three times: once before the pan is transferred to the oven, again after 20 minutes of baking, and once more before unmolding.

- Remember what you're looking for: a brown, crisp bottom in the pan. (The cake is flipped out of the pan, so the bottom will become the top.) Be careful that the bottom does not get too dark; you can peek, lifting up the cake slightly with an offset spatula or butter knife. You also want all of the potatoes to be cooked through, but to maintain a bit of texture (they should not be completely mushy or too soft to the touch). The top does not need to be golden as long as the potatoes are cooked through.

FINISHING AND SERVING

- Unmold the potatoes by running a spatula around the pan rim. Try to get the spatula under the potatoes, too, making sure they are not stuck to the bottom of the pan. Once you feel confident the potatoes can unmold, quickly turn the baking dish over onto a large serving platter. Or, if it makes you feel more comfortable, you can put a serving platter on top of the pan, and flip the pan

NOTES

over so the potato cake falls onto the platter. (Use oven mitts; the pan will be hot.) If some potato slices stick, remove them with the spatula and place them on top of the cake.

• If the dish looks like a disaster, follow Julia Child's advice: Cover the cake with grated Gruyère, Parmesan or Cheddar cheese, dot with another spoonful of butter, then brown for a few seconds under the broiler. The cheese will mask any imperfections.

• You can make pommes Anna up to 4 hours ahead. After draining the excess butter from the pan and unmolding the cake, flip it back in the pan and cover it. Place over a very low flame and reheat before serving.

Variations

Served plain, without embellishment, pommes Anna is a stunning dish. But after mastering its most basic form, you can take liberties with the recipe, adding cheeses, herbs and spices, and other vegetables.

CHEESE Adding cheese gives you a more intensely flavored dish with a melting, gooey center. And if you're using low-starch potatoes like all-purpose white or Yukon gold, the cheese acts as an adhesive, helping to glue the cake together. Add 6 ounces Gruyère, Cheddar or Emmental cheese, grated, along with (or instead of) the garlic. Make sure the cheese doesn't touch the bottom or sides of the pan or it can burn. You can also experiment with crumbled feta, blue cheese or goat cheese.

VEGETABLES Potatoes aren't the only vegetable that you can prepare in this fashion—other root vegetables and squashes will also work. Be sure to choose vegetables with a low moisture content so you get a crisp, browned exterior. Try sweet potatoes, turnips, winter squash, beets or rutabaga instead of (or in combination with) regular potatoes.

CHILES, HERBS AND SPICES For a bolder take on pommes Anna, substitute a thinly sliced shallot for the garlic, or add it along with the garlic. You could do the same with a sliced chile. You could also add a few tablespoons of chopped fresh herbs, such as tarragon, thyme, rosemary, sage or chives, or a dusting of nutmeg, cinnamon, cumin, fennel or other spices. Sprinkle herbs and spices on top of each layer of along with the salt and pepper.

Cassoulet

cass·ou·let | kas·oo·lā'
A sumptuous casserole of beans baked
slowly with cured and roasted meats.

Why Master It?

Cassoulet is one of the most magnificent examples of French home cooking. The sumptuous meat and bean casserole is not as refined as some of the fussier dishes of haute cuisine, but what it lacks in opulence it makes up for in rustic charm.

WE MAY THINK OF IT AS DECADENT, but cassoulet is at heart a humble bean and meat stew, rooted in the rural cooking of the Languedoc region. For urban dwellers without access to the staples of a farm in southwest France—crocks of rendered lard and poultry fat, vats of duck confit, hunks of meat from just-butchered pigs and lambs—preparing one is an epic undertaking. The reward, though, may well be the pinnacle of French home cooking.

Cassoulet does take time to make: There is overnight marinating and soaking, plus a long afternoon of roasting and simmering, and a few days on top of that if you make your own confit. However, it welcomes variation and leaves room for the personality of the cook—perhaps more than any other recipe in the canon. As long as you have white beans slowly stewed with some combination of sausages, pork, lamb, duck or goose, you have a cassoulet.

The hardest part about making a cassoulet when you're not in France is shopping for the ingredients. You will need to plan ahead, ordering the duck fat and confit and the garlic sausage online or from a good butcher, and finding sources for salt pork and fresh, bone-in pork and lamb stew meat. The beans, though, aren't hard to procure. Great Northern and cannellini beans make fine substitutes for the Tarbais, flageolet and lingot beans used in France.

Then give yourself over to the rhythm of roasting, sautéing and long, slow simmering. The final stew, a glorious pot of velvety beans and chunks of tender meat covered by a burnished crust, is well worth the effort.

"The Kitchen Table" by Jean-Baptiste-Siméon Chardin (1699–1779).

A Brief History

NAMED FOR THE CASSOLE, the earthenware pot in which it is traditionally cooked, cassoulet evolved over the centuries in the countryside of southwest France, changing with the ingredients on hand and the cooks stirring the pot.

The earliest versions were probably influenced by Spain, with its own ancient tradition of fava bean and meat stews. As the stew migrated to the Languedoc region, the fava beans were replaced by white beans, brought over from the Americas in the 16th century.

Three major towns of the region—Castelnaudary, Carcassonne and Toulouse—all vigorously lay claim to having created what they consider to be the only true cassoulet. It is a feud that has been going on at least since the middle of the 19th century.

In 1938, the chef Prosper Montagné, an author of the first version of "Larousse Gastronomique," attempted to resolve the dispute calling cassoulet "the god of Occidental cuisine" and likening the three competing versions to the Holy Trinity. The cassoulet from Castelnaudary, considered the oldest, is the Father in Montagné's trinity, made from a combination of beans, duck confit and pork (sausages, skin, knuckles, salt pork and roasted meat). The Carcassonne style is the Son, with mutton and the occasional partridge. The version from Toulouse, the Holy Spirit, was the first to add goose confit.

The recipe for cassoulet was codified by the "États Généraux de la Gastronomie" in 1966 in a way that allowed all three towns to claim authenticity. It said that to be called cassoulet, a stew must have at least 30 percent pork, mutton or preserved duck or goose (or a combination), and 70 percent white beans and stock, pork rinds, herbs and flavorings.

But two other main points of contention still inspire debate: the use of tomatoes and other vegetables with the beans, and a topping of bread crumbs that crisp in the oven. The beauty of it is that if you make your own cassoulet, you get to decide.

CASSOULET **133**

Cassoulet

YIELD 12 SERVINGS | **TIME** 5½ HOURS, PLUS MARINATING

This slow-cooked casserole requires a good deal of culinary stamina. But the voluptuous combination of aromatic beans with rich chunks of duck confit, sausage, pork and lamb is worth the effort. Serve it with a green salad. It doesn't need any other accompaniment, and you wouldn't have room for one anyway.

FOR THE MEAT

2½ pounds bone-in pork stew meat, cut into 2-inch pieces

2½ pounds bone-in lamb stew meat, cut into 2-inch pieces

2½ teaspoons kosher salt

9 garlic cloves, peeled, plus 3 grated or minced garlic cloves

⅛ teaspoon ground cloves

1 teaspoon freshly ground black pepper

1 bay leaf, torn into pieces

2 sprigs rosemary, torn into pieces

2 sprigs thyme, torn into pieces

½ cup/4 ounces duck fat, melted (or goose fat or lard, or a combination)

(continued on page 136)

STEP 1 | The night before cooking, marinate the meat and soak the beans. For meat: In a large bowl, combine meat, 2½ teaspoons salt, 9 peeled and 3 grated garlic cloves, ground cloves, 1 teaspoon black pepper, bay leaf, rosemary and thyme; and toss to combine. Cover and refrigerate overnight. For beans: In a large bowl, combine beans, 1 teaspoon salt and enough cold water to cover by 4 inches. Cover and let sit overnight.

STEP 2 | The next day, roast the meat: Heat oven to 325 degrees. Pour fat over meat in the bowl and toss to coat. Spread meat in one even layer on a rimmed baking sheet, leaving space between each piece to encourage browning (use two pans if necessary). Top meat with any fat left in bowl. Roast until browned, about 1 hour, then turn pieces, cover with foil, and continue to roast until soft, another 1½ hours. Remove meat from baking sheet, then scrape up all browned bits stuck to the pan. Reserve fat and browned bits.

STEP 3 | Meanwhile, cook the beans: Drain beans, add them to a large stockpot and cover with 2 inches water. Add bouquet garni, 1 stalk celery, 1 carrot, 2 garlic cloves, 2 teaspoons salt and ½ teaspoon pepper. Stick whole clove

CASSOULET **135**

Cassoulet | CONTINUED

FOR THE BEANS

1 pound dried Tarbais, flageolet, lingot, Great Northern or cannellini beans

3 teaspoons kosher salt

1 bouquet garni (3 sprigs Italian parsley, 3 sprigs thyme and 1 bay leaf, tied with kitchen string; see Techniques)

1 stalk celery, halved

1 large carrot, halved

2 garlic cloves, peeled

½ teaspoon freshly ground black pepper

1 whole clove

½ white onion, cut stem to root end

8 ounces fully cooked French garlic sausage or kielbasa, skin removed and cut into chunks

FOR THE REST

8 ounces salt pork

¼ cup duck fat (or goose fat, lard, a combination or olive oil), more as needed

1 pound fresh pork sausage, pricked all over with a fork

1½ large onions, diced

into the folds of the onion half and add that as well. Bring to a boil and then simmer over medium heat, stirring often, until beans are cooked through, 1 to 1½ hours, adding garlic sausage after 30 minutes. When beans are cooked, discard bouquet garni and aromatics, including vegetables. Reserving cooking liquid, drain the beans and sausage.

STEP 4 | While beans are cooking, bring a medium pot of water to a boil and add salt pork. Simmer for 30 minutes, remove and let cool. Cut off skin, then slice pork into very thin pieces and reserve.

STEP 5 | Heat a very large skillet (at least 12 inches) over medium heat and add a drizzle of duck or other fat. Add fresh pork sausages and cook until well browned on all sides, about 20 minutes. Remove to a plate and reserve, leaving any sausage fat in skillet.

STEP 6 | In same skillet over medium-high heat, add ¼ cup of the reserved fat and the browned bits from the roasted meat. Add diced onions, carrots and celery, and cook until softened, about 10 minutes. Add 9 whole garlic cloves and cook until fragrant, 2 to 4 minutes. Add tomato purée, season with salt to taste, and simmer until thickened to a saucelike consistency, 5 to 10 minutes, if necessary. Add cooked beans and stir to combine. Remove from heat and reserve.

STEP 7 | Assemble the cassoulet: Heat oven to 375 degrees. In a large Dutch oven, lay salt pork pieces in an even layer to cover the bottom of the pot. Add a scant third of the bean and garlic sausage mixture, spreading evenly. Top with half of the roasted meat pieces, 2 pork sausages and 2 duck legs. Add

2 large carrots, diced

2 celery stalks, diced

9 garlic cloves, peeled

3 cups tomato purée, from fresh or canned tomatoes

Kosher salt, to taste

4 legs duck confit, bought or homemade (see Techniques)

1½ cups panko or other plain, dried bread crumbs

another scant third of the bean mixture, and top with remaining meat, sausages and duck legs. Top with remaining beans, spreading them to the edges and covering all meat. Pour reserved bean liquid along the edges of the pot, until liquid comes up to the top layer of beans but does not cover. Sprinkle bread crumbs on top and drizzle with ¼ cup duck fat.

STEP 8 | Bake until crust is lightly browned, about 30 minutcs. Use a large spoon to lightly crack the crust; the bean liquid will bubble up. Use the spoon to drizzle the bean liquid all over the top of the crust. Return to oven and bake 1 hour more, cracking the crust and drizzling with the bean liquid every 20 minutes, until the crust is well browned and liquid is bubbling. (The total baking time should be 1½ hours.) Remove from oven and let cool slightly, then serve.

Equipment You'll Need

Cassoulet is a hearty dish and requires a hearty pot. Be sure it isn't too heavy to lift when it's full.

CASSEROLE DISH You will need a deep casserole dish that holds at least eight quarts, or a large Dutch oven, to bake the cassoulet. If you use a Dutch oven, you won't need the cover. The cassoulet needs to bake uncovered to develop a crisp crust.

BAKING SHEETS All of the ingredients for a cassoulet are cooked before being combined and baked again. The meat can be cooked in any number of ways; here, the pork and lamb stew meat is roasted on rimmed baking sheets so that it browns.

LARGE POT The beans and garlic sausage (or kielbasa) are cooked in a large pot before they are added to the casserole, though you could use a slow cooker or pressure cooker, if you have one. You will also need a second small pot for simmering the salt pork.

Techniques and Tips

The hardest part of making a cassoulet may be obtaining the ingredients. Beyond that, it helps to think of cooking and building it in stages. Once you've gathered and prepared the components (the meat, beans, salt pork, sausage, duck confit and bread crumb topping), assembling the dish is just a matter of layering the elements.

SHOPPING FOR INGREDIENTS

• You can use any kind of roasted meats for a cassoulet, and the kinds vary by region. Substitute roasted chicken, turkey or goose for the duck confit, bone-in beef for the lamb and bone-in veal for the pork. Lamb neck is a great substitute for the bone-in lamb stew meat, and you can use any chunks of bone-in pork, like pork ribs, in place of the pork stew meat. (The bones give the dish more flavor, and their gelatin helps thicken the final stew.)

• Do not use smoked sausages in the beans, and don't substitute smoked bacon for the salt pork. The smoky flavor can overwhelm the dish, and it is not traditional in French cassoulets. If you can't find salt pork, pancetta will work in its place, and you won't need to poach it beforehand.

• You can buy duck confit at gourmet markets or order it online. If you'd prefer to make it yourself, this is how to do it: Rub 4 fresh duck legs with a

NOTES

large pinch of salt each. Place in a dish and generously sprinkle with whole peppercorns, thyme sprigs and smashed, peeled garlic cloves. Cover and let cure for 4 to 24 hours in the refrigerator. When ready to cook, wipe the meat dry with paper towels, discarding the garlic, pepper and herbs. Place in a Dutch oven or baking dish and cover completely with fat. (Duck fat is traditional, but olive oil also works.) Bake in a 200-degree oven until the duck is tender and well browned, 3 to 4 hours. Let duck cool in the fat before refrigerating. Duck confit lasts for at least a month in the refrigerator and tastes best after sitting for 1 week. Try it warm, over noodles or a salad, or with eggs.

• Don't think the meat is the only star of this dish. The beans need just as much love. You want them velvety, sitting in a trove of tomato, stock and rich fat. Buy the best beans you can, preferably ones that have been harvested and dried within a year of cooking. The variety of white bean is less important than their freshness. Canned beans will become mushy.

• Bread crumbs aren't traditional for cassoulet, but will result in a topping with an especially airy and crisp texture. Regular dried bread crumbs, either bought or homemade, will also work.

• Use a sharp knife to cut off all the skin of the salt pork and to slice it thinly.

NOTES

COOKING THE PARTS AND ASSEMBLING THE DISH

• When you roast the meat, leave plenty of space between the chunks of meat so they brown nicely. More browning means richer flavor. You can also use leftover roasted meat if you have some on hand.

• The bouquet garni flavors both the beans and the bean liquid, which is used to moisten the cassoulet as it bakes. To make one, take sprigs of parsley and thyme and a bay leaf and tie them together with at least 1 foot of kitchen string. Tuck the bay leaf in the middle of the bouquet and make sure you wrap the herbs up thoroughly, several times around, so they don't escape into the pot.

• Feel free to use a slow cooker or pressure cooker for the beans. Add the garlic sausage (or kielbasa) about halfway through the cooking time. It doesn't have to be exact, since the sausage is already cooked; you're adding it to flavor the beans and their liquid.

• Use a very large skillet, at least 12 inches, for sautéing the sausages and finishing the beans before you layer them into the casserole dish.

• In this recipe, the beans are finished in a tomato purée, which reduces and thickens the sauce of the final cassoulet. But you can substitute a good homemade stock for the purée. You'll get a soupier cassoulet, but it's just as traditional without the tomatoes.

NOTES

- The salt pork is layered in strips into the bottom of the baking dish. Then, while cooking, it crisps and turns into a bottom crust for the stew. So it is important to slice it thinly and carefully place it in a single layer on the bottom of the dish (and up the sides, if you have enough). Don't overlap it very much, or those parts won't get as crisp.

- The reserved bean liquid is added to the cassoulet for cooking, and its starchiness is what keeps the stew thick and creamy. Using stock instead would make for a soupier but still delicious cassoulet.

NOTES

• Create a substantial top crust with crunch by repeatedly cracking the thick layer of bread crumbs as the cassoulet cooks, and by drizzling the topping with bean liquid, which browns and crisps in the heat. It's best to crack the topping in even little taps with the side of a large spoon. You want to create more texture and crunch by exposing more of the bread crumbs to the hot oven and bean liquid, which should be drizzled generously and evenly.

• If you like, you can skip the bread crumbs entirely, which is just as traditional. The top will brown on its own, but there won't be a texturally distinct crust.

• You can break up the work, cooking the separate elements ahead of time and reserving them until you are ready to layer and bake the cassoulet. Or assemble the cassoulet in its entirety ahead of time, without bread crumbs, and then top and bake just before serving.

Soufflé

---

souf·fle | soo-flā

An airy baked dish that combines beaten egg whites with a flavorful base.

Why Master It?

A hallmark of French cooking, the soufflé is
like magic. It uses nothing more than air to transform
workaday eggs into a lofty masterpiece, puffing
and browning in the oven before collapsing at first bite.

IN "MASTERING THE ART OF FRENCH COOKING," their profoundly influential 1961 cookbook, Julia
Child, Simone Beck and Louisette Bertholle describe the soufflé as the "epitome and triumph
of the art of French cooking." A half-century later, soufflé remains as vital as ever, as successive generations of chefs revisit and refresh the classic recipe.

A soufflé has two main components, a flavorful base and glossy beaten egg whites, and
they are gently folded together just before baking. The word itself comes from "souffler," meaning "to breathe" or "to puff," which is what the whites do to the base once they hit the oven's heat.

The base may be made either savory or sweet. Savory soufflés usually incorporate cheese,
vegetables, meat or seafood and are appropriate for a light dinner or lunch, or as a first course.
They require a substantial and stable base, in the form of a cooked sauce that often involves
butter, egg yolks and some kind of starch (flour, rice or cornstarch). Sweet soufflés, with fruit,
chocolate or liquors, make spectacular desserts. The base can be made from a fruit purée, or a
sweet, rich sauce. More sauce, complementing or contrasting, can be added for serving.

Soufflés are found all over France, with each region applying its own spin. In Alsace,
cooks use kirsch. In Provence, goat cheese or eggplant are excellent additions. And naturally,
Roquefort cheese is a popular addition in Roquefort.

SOUFFLÉ **147**

The menu cover at Le Soufflé, a restaurant in Paris.

A Brief History

MARIE-ANTOINE CARÊME, THE FATHER OF FRENCH HAUTE CUISINE, is credited with perfecting and popularizing the soufflé, publishing his recipe in "Le Pâtissier Royal Parisien" in 1815. (The first recipe had appeared in 1742, in Vincent La Chapelle's "Le Cuisinier Moderne.") Initially, Carême made his soufflés in stiff pastry casings called croustades that were lined with buttered paper. Soon after, vessels were developed just for making soufflés, deep dishes with straight sides, for the tallest rise. Carême went on to create several variations, including Soufflé Rothschild, named after his employer, one of the richest men in France; it contained candied fruit macerated in a liquor containing flecks of gold. (Contemporary versions substitute more attainable kirsch for the golden elixir.)

As the soufflé evolved, the number of variations grew. By the time Auguste Escoffier published "Le Guide Culinaire" in 1903, which codified the classic recipes of French cuisine, more than 60 soufflé variations were in common use, with versions that incorporated ingredients as diverse as Parmesan cheese, foie gras, escarole, pheasant, violets, almonds and tea. A layered soufflé called a Camargo alternated stripes of tangerine and hazelnut soufflé batters in the same dish. "Mastering the Art of French Cooking," published nearly six decades later, offered several recipes, including a version called Soufflé Vendôme, in which cold poached eggs are layered into the unbaked soufflé mixture. After baking, the eggs warm up slightly, releasing their runny yolks when the soufflé is broken.

Despite a movement in France in recent years that called for a more experimental take on traditional cuisine, there is still a place for a perfect soufflé. And while chefs may innovate upon the classic version, those first 18th-century recipes are still very much in use.

SOUFFLÉ **149**

Bittersweet Chocolate Soufflé

YIELD 6 SERVINGS | **TIME** 45 MINUTES

A chocolate soufflé is an eternal showstopper of a dessert. The flavor is dark and intense, yet the texture is light and custardy. Be sure to use excellent bittersweet chocolate. For maximum drama, always serve a soufflé straight from the oven.

½ cup/114 grams unsalted butter (1 stick), softened, plus more for coating dish

4 tablespoons/50 grams granulated sugar, plus more for coating dish

8 ounces/225 grams bittersweet chocolate (60 to 65 percent cacao), finely chopped

6 eggs, separated, at room temperature

Pinch fine sea salt

½ teaspoon cream of tartar

STEP 1 | Remove wire racks from oven and place a baking sheet directly on oven floor. Heat oven to 400 degrees. Generously butter a 1 ½-quart soufflé dish. Coat bottom and sides thoroughly with sugar, tapping out excess. Make sure sugar covers all the butter on the sides of the dish.

STEP 2 | In a medium bowl, melt chocolate and butter either in the microwave or in a bowl over a pot of simmering water. Let cool only slightly, then whisk in egg yolks and salt.

STEP 3 | Using an electric mixer, beat egg whites and cream of tartar at medium speed until the mixture is fluffy and holds very soft peaks. Add sugar, 1 tablespoon at a time, beating until whites hold stiff peaks and look glossy.

STEP 4 | Gently whisk a quarter of the egg whites into the chocolate mixture to lighten it. Fold in remaining whites in two additions, then transfer batter to prepared dish. Rub your thumb around the inside edge of the dish to create about a ¼-inch space between the dish and the soufflé mixture.

STEP 5 | Put dish on baking sheet in the oven, and reduce oven to 375 degrees. Bake until soufflé is puffed and center moves slightly when shaken gently, 25 to 35 minutes. (Don't open oven door during first 20 minutes.) Less time makes a runnier soufflé; more time makes a firmer one. Serve immediately.

SOUFFLÉ

Equipment You'll Need

Chances are, you already have a straight-sided, ceramic soufflé dish. If not, it's a versatile investment.

SOUFFLÉ MOLD The soufflé has a pan created just for it, a deep ceramic dish with straight sides. Ceramic holds the heat evenly, so the center cooks at nearly the same rate as the edges, and the sides direct the expanding air upward, to give the most rise. A heavy metal charlotte mold also works. Or use a shallow oven-safe dish, like a gratin dish or a skillet. The soufflé won't rise as high, but it will still puff up. (It will likely cook faster, so watch it carefully.)

METAL MIXING BOWL You will achieve better results beating the whites in a metal mixing bowl rather than in a plastic, glass or ceramic bowl. Plastic can retain oily residue, and glass and ceramic are slippery, making it harder to get the whites to cling and climb up the sides. This is especially important if you are beating the whites by hand. Stainless steel or copper work best.

ELECTRIC MIXER Using an electric mixer, whether it is a hand-held model or a stand mixer, makes the work of beating egg whites go faster and easier than if you were to use a whisk and your arms.

Techniques and Tips

The primary technique for making a tall and airy soufflé is the proper beating of the egg whites to make first soft peaks, then stiff ones. Once you learn it, a whole fluffy world of spongecakes, mousses and foams.

NOTES

SEPARATING THE EGGS

- Always use eggs at room temperature or even warm, for the highest rise. Cold egg whites won't beat up as loftily. To get cold eggs to temperature quickly, soak them in their shells in warm water for 20 minutes.

- Make sure your hands are clean. If there is any trace of oil or grease on them and you touch the egg whites, the soufflé may not puff.

- Crack your eggs on a flat surface, like the countertop, instead of on the rim of the bowl. That way, you are less likely to shatter the shell and pierce the yolk.

- There are two ways to separate eggs. The first is to hold the cracked egg over a bowl and pass the yolk between shells, letting the white slip into the bowl. Gently drop the yolk into a separate, smaller bowl. Take care: The sharp edge of the shell can easily pierce the yolk, allowing it to seep into the white.

The other method requires you to strain the whites through your fingers, but it ensures that yolks do not creep into the whites. First, set up 3 bowls.

SOUFFLÉ 153

NOTES

Hold your hand over one bowl and drop the cracked egg into your palm, letting the white run through your fingers into the bowl. Drop the yolk into the second bowl. Inspect the white for traces of yolk. If there are none, slip the white into the third bowl. Repeat with remaining eggs. Using that first bowl as a way station for each freshly cracked white before it gets added to the main bowl of pristine whites helps ensure that no yolk contaminates the mixture.

BEATING THE WHITES

- Well-beaten, stable whites are the key to a gorgeously puffy soufflé. So don't rush this step. The slower you go, the better your chances for success.

- Take a moment to make sure there are no traces of yolk or any fat in the egg whites or the bowl. (Egg yolk will impede the whites from frothing.)

- Adding a little bit of acid (in our recipes, cream of tartar) helps stabilize the egg foam, and also helps prevent overbeating. Beating the whites in a copper bowl will produce a similar result without the added acid, which is why copper bowls were historically considered essential for making meringues.

- If you are using a stand mixer, check the bottom of the bowl every now and then for unbeaten egg whites. Sometimes the whites pool there, and when you go to incorporate the meringue into the base, those whites will deflate the overall soufflé. Whisk any pooled whites by hand into the rest of the meringue and continue beating with the machine until very soft peaks form.

- Add sugar gradually (if using) and beat until the meringue is just able to hold stiff peaks. This means that when you lift the whisk out of the meringue, it will create a little cowlick that stays upright without drooping as you gently move the whisk. It should look glossy, or be just starting to lose its shine. Don't overbeat (which will make the foam turn grainy and dry) or underbeat (which won't give the proper lift). If you overbeat your whites, beating in another egg white often restores them.

NOTES

COMBINING THE WHITES AND THE BASE

- The goal in folding the egg whites into the base is to work quickly and use a light touch. This lightens the base, making it easier to fold in the rest of the meringue mixture all at once. Using a rubber spatula, fold in a C shape: Starting in the middle of the bowl, drag the thin edge of a spatula down like a knife, then tilt and scoop up a spatula full of the soufflé base, making sure to scrape the bottom of the bowl. Turn the batter over, away from your body, back into the middle of the bowl. Shift the bowl 45 degrees, and repeat.

- Stop folding when the streaks of white have just disappeared—or rather, when they have almost disappeared. A few white streaks are preferable to overfolding, which deflates the batter.

BAKING THE SOUFFLÉ

- Buttering the soufflé dish, then coating the butter with something with a bit of texture, is essential for the rise. If the soufflé dish were to be just buttered,

NOTES

the soufflé would slip down the sides instead of climbing. An additional thin coating of granulated sugar, bread crumbs, ground nuts or grated cheese creates a rough texture for the egg whites to hold onto as they rise.

• If your soufflé dish isn't big enough to accommodate all of the batter, you can extend it by tying a buttered piece of parchment paper or foil around the rim of the soufflé dish to increase its volume.

• For individual soufflés, use small ramekins placed on a rimmed baking sheet so they are easy to get in and out of the oven. Reduce the cooking time of a larger soufflé by about half.

• Heat matters. Make sure the oven is preheated: that initial hot blast expands the air trapped inside the bubbly foam of batter, which makes it rise. Having the soufflé base hot or warm when you fold in the egg whites helps the temperature rise quickly, too.

• Baking the soufflé on a preheated baking sheet on the bottom of the oven helps the soufflé cook on the bottom as well as the top, producing a more even result. The baking sheet will also catch any overflow.

• For a higher rise, rub your thumb around the inside rim of the soufflé dish to create a gap between the dish and the batter. (Many soufflé dishes already have a groove there to help.)

NOTES

• If you want a perfectly flat top to your soufflé, level the foam with the back of a knife before baking, and before running your thumb around the edge of the dish. Or you could leave the foam as it is, for a more natural, wavy look. Julia Child preferred a natural top; pastry chefs tend to prefer a flat top.

• A soufflé is done baking when it has risen above the rim of the dish and is nicely browned on top. It should feel mostly firm and only slightly jiggly when you lightly tap the top. Flourless soufflés, such as those made with fruit purée or chocolate, are lighter and cook faster. (Chocolate soufflés can also be intentionally underbaked for a gooey chocolate interior. The soufflé should be a tad wiggly when gently shaken but firm around the edges.) Thicker soufflés made with flour, like a cheese soufflé, don't rise as much in the oven, but won't collapse as much either.

• Use the window of your oven to monitor the soufflé, and don't open the oven door until you see the soufflé puff up over the sides of the dish. Once it has done that, you can safely open the oven and check on it.

• If the top of your soufflé starts to brown too fast, top it with a round of parchment paper.

• All soufflés fall within minutes of coming out of the oven, because the hot air bubbles contract when they hit cooler air. That's why you need to serve them immediately after baking. But as long as you don't overfold the whites, and you resist opening the oven door until the last few minutes of baking, your soufflé will rise gloriously before the dramatic and expected collapse.

• You can prepare any soufflé batter ahead, but you will probably lose some volume. Assemble the soufflé in its dish, then set it aside in a warm place without drafts for up to four hours. Julia Child recommended turning your largest soup pot over the soufflé, and that would work. But any draft-free space is fine. A draft could deflate the foam.

Variation: Gruyère and Chive Soufflé

YIELD 6 SERVINGS | **TIME** 45 MINUTES

This savory soufflé is as classic as can be, with beaten egg whites folded into a rich, cheese-laden béchamel for flavor and stability. Gruyère is the traditional cheese used for soufflé, but a good aged Cheddar would also work nicely. This makes a great lunch or brunch dish.

3 tablespoons/42 grams unsalted butter, plus more for coating dish

5 tablespoons/25 grams finely grated Parmesan cheese

1 cup whole milk

3 tablespoons all-purpose flour

½ teaspoon paprika

¼ teaspoon fine sea salt

Pinch ground nutmeg

4 large egg yolks

5 large egg whites

½ teaspoon cream of tartar

1 cup/115 grams coarsely grated Gruyère cheese

2 tablespoons chopped chives

STEP 1 | Remove wire racks from oven and place a baking sheet directly on oven floor. Heat oven to 400 degrees. Butter a 1½-quart soufflé dish. Coat bottom and sides with 3 tablespoons/17 grams Parmesan, tapping out any excess.

STEP 2 | In a small pot, heat milk until steaming. Meanwhile, melt butter in a large skillet over medium heat. Whisk in flour and cook until the mixture foams, about 3 minutes. Remove from heat and whisk in warm milk. Return to heat and cook until thickened, whisking constantly, about 3 minutes.

STEP 3 | Remove from heat and whisk in paprika, salt and nutmeg. Whisk in egg yolks one at a time, blending fully after each addition. Transfer flour and yolk mixture to a large bowl.

STEP 4 | Using an electric mixer, beat egg whites and cream of tartar at medium speed until the mixture holds stiff peaks.

STEP 5 | Whisk a quarter of the whites into the lukewarm yolk mixture to lighten. Gently fold in remaining whites in 2 additions while gradually sprinkling in Gruyère cheese, remaining 2 tablespoons Parmesan and the chives. Transfer batter to prepared dish. Rub your thumb around the inside edge of the dish to create a ¼-inch or so space between the dish and the soufflé mixture.

STEP 6 | Transfer dish to baking sheet in the oven and reduce oven temperature to 375 degrees. Bake until soufflé is puffed and golden brown on top and center barely moves when dish is shaken gently, about 30 minutes. (Do not open oven door during first 20 minutes.) Bake it a little less for a runnier soufflé and a little more for a firmer soufflé. Serve immediately.

Variation: Red Berry Soufflé

YIELD 6 SERVINGS | **TIME** 45 MINUTES

Once you've mastered more basic soufflés, try this very light recipe, adapted from Julia Child, which uses a base of syrupy fruit to flavor the egg whites, without the addition of fats or starches. A combination of raspberries and strawberries makes it marvelously pink.

Unsalted butter, for dish

1 cup and 2 tablespoons/228 grams sugar, plus more for coating the dish

1¾ cups/227 grams/ 8 ounces fresh strawberries, washed, hulled and quartered

1⅔ cups/227 grams/ 8 ounces fresh raspberries

1 tablespoon balsamic vinegar

¼ teaspoon cream of tartar

Finely grated zest of 1 lemon

4 large egg whites

Pinch salt

STEP 1 | Remove wire racks from oven and place a baking sheet directly on oven floor. Heat oven to 425 degrees. Generously butter a 1½-quart soufflé dish. Coat bottom and sides thoroughly with sugar, tapping out excess. To get the best rise, make sure there is sugar covering all of the butter on the sides of the dish.

STEP 2 | In a medium bowl, toss berries with ⅓ cup sugar and vinegar. Let stand for at least 30 minutes.

STEP 3 | Drain berries in a sieve set over a bowl, reserving juices. If less than ¼ cup, add water to total ¼ cup liquid.

STEP 4 | In a small saucepan, combine ⅔ cup sugar with berry juices. Bring to a boil over high heat, swirling occasionally, until sugar is completely dissolved. Cover pan and continue to boil until sugar reaches 235 degrees on a candy thermometer (soft ball stage), about 1 minute.

STEP 5 | Fold drained berries into hot syrup and bring mixture back to a boil, about 1 minute. Drain berries again, reserving juices. Return juices to the saucepan and boil until thickened, adding any accumulated juices in the bowl of berries, about 3 minutes. Remove from heat, fold in berries and lemon zest, and set aside to thicken and cool slightly.

SOUFFLÉ **161**

Red Berry Soufflé | CONTINUED

STEP 6 | In the bowl of an electric mixer, beat egg whites until foamy. Add salt and cream of tartar and gradually increase speed to high. Add remaining 2 tablespoons sugar, a tablespoon at a time, and continue beating until egg whites hold stiff, glossy peaks. Immediately add berry mixture to one side of the bowl and quickly but delicately fold together. Transfer batter to prepared dish. Rub your thumb around the inside edge of the dish to create about a ¼-inch space between the dish and the soufflé mixture.

STEP 7 | Transfer dish to baking sheet in the oven. Bake until soufflé is puffed and center moves only slightly when shaken gently, about 10 to 12 minutes. Bake it a little less for a runnier soufflé and a little more for a firmer one. Serve immediately.

Serving Sweet Soufflés

Savory soufflés are usually served by themselves, but sweet soufflés often have a sauce on the side, to be poured into the center of the soufflé after you've dug in your spoon. Or opt for ice cream, which provides a thrilling hot-cold contrast. Either will deflate the soufflé, so add it after your guests have had a chance to admire it.

CRÈME ANGLAIS This creamy custard, made from egg yolks and milk, is a great sauce for any sweet soufflé, including chocolate, fruit and Grand Marnier. You can flavor the sauce with a dash of liquor, some lemon zest or a pinch of cinnamon or another spice.

CARAMEL SAUCE A versatile choice, caramel sauce is lovely with all kinds of sweet soufflés, be they flavored with simple vanilla bean, chocolate or fruit.

FRUIT SAUCE A perfect match for fruit soufflés, this can be as simple as a lightly sweetened purée of fruit, or a more elaborate fruit-flavored custard or curd.

CHOCOLATE SAUCE A chocolate sauce accentuates the richness of chocolate soufflés. You can use the same type of chocolate in the sauce as you've used in the soufflé, or try mixing it up, using a darker and more bitter chocolate to cut the sweetness, or a milk chocolate to step it up.

The New York Times
Cooking

MELISSA CLARK is a reporter for The New York Times Food department, where she writes a cooking column, creates recipes and appears in a weekly video series. Melissa is the author of 38 cookbooks, including her latest, "Dinner: Changing the Game," and collaborations with two of New York's most celebrated French chefs, Daniel Boulud and David Bouley. Born and raised in Brooklyn, she spent her childhood summers in France with her family, where she learned about French food firsthand. She is working on her next book, "First We Get Lost, Then We Have Lunch," which will chronicle her experiences eating and cooking in France.

EXPERIENCE A NEW KIND OF COOKBOOK
The recipes and stories on these pages are just the beginning. Visit NYT Cooking for additional videos and step-by-step instruction, as well as for more than 18,000 recipes from around the world. **nytcooking.com**

Design by Barbara de Wilde and Mary Jane Callister

All Photographs by Francesco Tonelli except pages 22, 23, 37, 53, 66, 67, 111, 127, 163 by Karsten Moran.

Copyright © 2017 *The New York Times Company*. All rights reserved.

ISBN: 978-0-9995288-0-8